Young Charles Darwin AND THE VOYAGE OF THE BEAGLE

To Ernie

—R. A.

Published by
PEACHTREE PUBLISHERS
1700 Chattahoochee Avenue
Atlanta, Georgia 30318-2112
www.peachtree-online.com

Text © 2009 by Ruth Ashby
Illustrations © 2009 by Suzanne Duranceau

Book design by Loraine M. Joyner and Melanie McMahon Ives

Illustrations drawn by hand and digitally colorized. Text typeset in Bronte; title typeset in Oldgate Lane Outline; subtitle typeset in Bolton. Map fonts are Sidhe Noble and Garamond Classic.

Printed and bound in China
10 9 8 7 6 5 4 3 2 1
First Edition

Library of Congress Cataloging-in-Publication Data

Ashby, Ruth.
   Young Charles Darwin and the voyage of the Beagle / written by Ruth Ashby. -- 1st ed.
      p. cm.
   ISBN 13: 978-1-56145-478-5 / ISBN 10: 1-56145-478-8
   1. Darwin, Charles, 1809-1882.--Juvenile literature. 2. Beagle Expedition (1831-1836)--Juvenile literature. 3. Naturalist--England--Biography--Juvenile literature. 4. Voyages around the world--Juvenile literature. I. Title.
   QH31.D2.A797 2009
   910.4'1--dc22

                              2008036747

Young Charles Darwin AND THE VOYAGE OF THE BEAGLE

RUTH ASHBY

PEACHTREE
ATLANTA

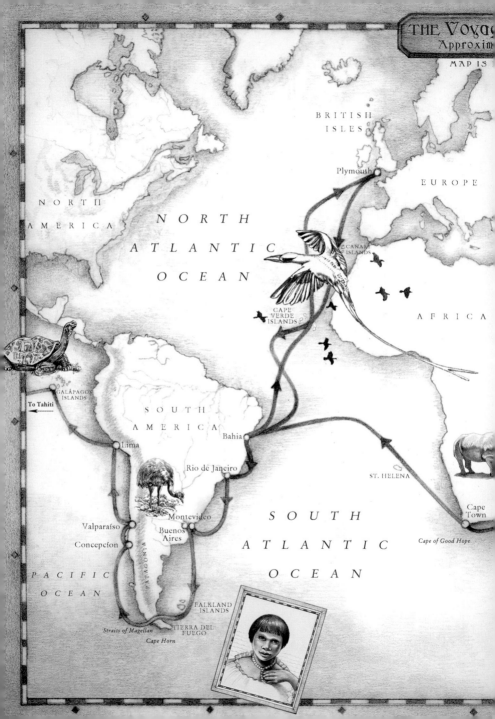

BRITISH
ISLES

Plymouth

EUROPE

NORTH
AMERICA

NORTH
ATLANTIC
OCEAN

CANARY
ISLANDS

AFRICA

CAPE
VERDE
ISLANDS

To Tahiti

GALÁPAGOS
ISLANDS

SOUTH
AMERICA

Bahia

Lima

Rio de Janeiro

ST. HELENA

Montevideo

Valparaíso

Buenos
Aires

SOUTH

Concepción

ATLANTIC

PACIFIC

OCEAN

Cape
Town

Cape of Good Hope

PATAGONIA

OCEAN

FALKLAND
ISLANDS

Straits of Magellan

TIERRA DEL
FUEGO

Cape Horn

E *Beagle*
31-1836
O SCALE

N
W E
S

ASIA

PACIFIC

OCEAN

INDIAN OCEAN

ADAGASCAR

MAURITIUS

King George Sound

AUSTRALIA

Sydney

TASMANIA

NEW
ZEALAND

TABLE OF CONTENTS

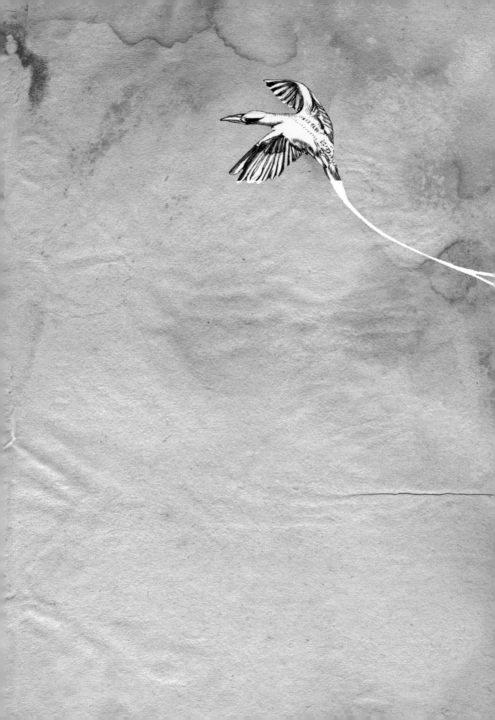

INTRODUCTION

The Chance of a Lifetime

A trip around the world! Twenty-three-year-old Charles Darwin couldn't believe his luck. He eagerly reread the letter from his friend and teacher, John Stevens Henslow:

> *August 24, 1831*
>
> *I shall hope to see you shortly fully expecting that you will eagerly catch at the offer which is likely to be made you of a trip to Terra del Fuego & home by the East Indies.... The Voyage is to last 2 yrs & if you take plenty of Books with you, anything you please may be done.... In short I suppose there never was a finer chance for a man of zeal & spirit.*

His excitement growing, Darwin read on. A ship captain named Robert FitzRoy was seeking a companion on a scientific voyage from Britain to the coast of

South America and across the Pacific Ocean to Australia and southeast Asia. The captain wanted a traveler who knew a lot about plants and animals and other aspects of natural history. He should be young. (FitzRoy himself was only twenty-six.) He should be a gentleman. And he should be ready for adventure!

"You are the very man they are looking for," Henslow insisted. Charles Darwin knew his friend was right. Darwin was a natural-born scientist, enthralled by the world of plants and animals. Even as a boy in the English countryside, he had eagerly collected flowers, butterflies, rocks, and birds. In college, where he was trained by some of the best biologists, botanists, and geologists in the country, he had searched for sponges and corals on the coast and gained a passion for collecting beetles.

Since graduating from Cambridge University the previous spring, Darwin had been searching for adventure. His father, Dr. Robert Darwin, had already decided that his son would enter the ministry and become a clergyman in a country church. But before he settled down, Charles longed to see the world. He planned to take a sea trip to the Canary Islands, off the coast of Africa, where he could explore tropical rain forests and climb the sides of an ancient volcano. But the arrangements fell through, and Charles had to make do instead with a walking tour of Wales to collect rock samples and prehistoric bones. When he returned on August 29, 1831, he found Henslow's letter waiting for him.

Charles's response was immediate. Of course he would go!

Not so fast, his father warned. The voyage would be long and dangerous. It would keep Charles from starting his career and making a living as a clergyman. It required an experienced naturalist, which Charles was not. And besides, his father pointed out, other more-qualified men had already been offered the position and turned it down. Clearly *they* knew that this so-called trip of a lifetime was nothing but a "wild scheme!"

Disheartened, Darwin wrote Henslow a sad refusal. "As far as my own mind is concerned, I should...*certainly* most gladly have accepted the opportunity, which you kindly have offered me. But my father, although he does not decidedly refuse me, gives such strong advice against going, that I should not be comfortable if I did not follow it."

Then his father threw him a lifeline.

"If you can find any man of common sense who

advises you to go," Dr. Darwin told his son, "I will give my consent."

Charles knew just the man—his Uncle Jos, a manufacturer who ran the famous family pottery business. Josiah Wedgwood was greatly respected for his kindliness and common sense. If his father listened to anyone, if would be Josiah.

Impulsively, Charles jumped on a horse and rode the twenty miles to Uncle Jos's estate. He outlined the plan to his uncle and his Wedgwood cousins. They thought it was a marvelous venture, not to be missed on any account. Josiah scribbled a letter to the doctor, dismissing Dr. Darwin's objections one by one. Most important of all was the flourish that ended the note. The voyage, Josiah wrote, would give his nephew "such an opportunity of seeing men and things as happens to few."

To Charles's intense joy, his father gave in. Charles Darwin would have his grand voyage!

The next few months were a blur of activity as Charles prepared for the voyage. There were supplies to buy, shipmates to meet, farewells to make to family and friends. Above all, he had to prepare himself mentally for the challenges to come. He was determined to make every moment count. "If I have not energy enough to make myself steadily industrious during the voyage," he wrote in his journal, "how great & uncommon an opportunity for improving myself shall I throw away. May this never for one moment escape my mind."

Finally, on December 27, 1831, HMS *Beagle* sailed out of Plymouth Harbor into the great unknown. What happened during the next five years has passed into legend. The observations that Charles Darwin made on the *Beagle* led to his development of the theory of evolution and to a new era in science. Years later, Darwin himself admitted,

> *The Voyage of the Beagle has been by far the most important event in my life and has determined my whole career.... I have always felt that I owe to the voyage the first real training or education of my mind; I was led to attend closely to several branches of natural history, and thus my powers of observation were improved....*

With this one spectacular voyage, Charles Darwin would transform the study of biology forever.

CHAPTER ONE
Songbirds and Sea Mats

No one who knew Charles Darwin as a boy ever thought he would grow up to be famous. They didn't even think he would be successful. "You care for nothing but shooting, dogs, and rat-catching," his father scolded him when he was about fifteen, "and you will be a disgrace to yourself and your family."

The Darwin family name was not to be taken lightly. Charles had quite a heritage to live up to. His two famous grandfathers had made the family both wealthy and respectable. His mother's father, the elder Josiah Wedgwood, had invented a new method for making pottery and had built a great and prosperous factory. His father's father, Erasmus Darwin, had been a doctor, an inventor, and a poet. In the late 1700s, when England was in the throes of a scientific and industrial revolution, both Wedgwood and the elder Darwin were on the cutting edge of change. Along with James Watt, the inventor of the steam engine, and Joseph Priestley, the discoverer of oxygen, they belonged to Birmingham's "Lunar Society." The members, known as the "Lunaticks," met once a month to discuss innovations in science and technology.

Erasmus even wrote a vast 1,400-page encyclopedia of information on medicine and animal life, called *Zoonomia*. Long before his grandson made a study of changes in nature, Erasmus Darwin used the word "evolution" in his writings.

When Erasmus's son Robert and Wedgwood's daughter Susannah married in April 1796, they settled down on a comfortable estate in Shrewsbury called The Mount. There they raised six children, four girls and two boys. The second son, Charles Robert Darwin, was born on February 12, 1809.

From the start, Charles tried to be the center of attention. A middle child who was often lost in the hubbub of a great house, he wanted above all to be noticed and admired. He collected birds' nests, shells, pebbles, and minerals, in part because he could show them off to others. At home, he stole peaches and plums so he could pretend to find them the next day. At school, he invented stories about birds and flowers, and boasted of being able to turn crocuses any color of the rainbow. "Inventing deliberate falsehoods became a regular method of seeking the spotlight," he remembered years later.

Suddenly, when Charles was eight, his mother died of cancer. He and his brother Erasmus (Ras) and younger sister Catherine were left in the care of their older sisters Marianne, Caroline, and Susan. Their father, Dr. Darwin, was depressed after the death of his wife. Though he was kind and considerate to his patients, he became ever stricter at home. At six-foot-two and more than three hundred pounds, Dr. Darwin inspired respect, awe, and perhaps a bit of fear in his younger son. Charles often fell short of pleasing his father. It didn't help that the boy was not much of a student. At the Shrewsbury School, Charles suffered under the burden of Greek and Latin, the traditional curriculum for an English gentleman. The long-dead languages bored him to death.

Charles escaped outdoors. He grew plants in his mother's greenhouse and gathered shells and strange insects. Strolling along the beach, he observed the swooping flight of gulls and cormorants. "I took much pleasure in watching the habits of birds, and even made notes on the subject. In my simplicity, I remember wondering why every gentleman did not become an ornithologist [bird scientist]." With Ras he rigged up a chemistry lab in the garden shed. Somehow "Gas" Darwin, as Charles's friends now called him, managed not to blow himself up.

He blasted away at other creatures, though. Charles received his first gun at age fifteen and was soon taking shots at snipe, quail, and partridge. From the start he enjoyed hunting, one of the favorite hobbies of the English country gentleman. "I do not believe that any-one could have shown more zeal for the most holy cause than I did for shooting birds," he remarked.

He would ride his horse over to the Wedgwood estate at Maer for shooting parties. Generous, easy-going Uncle Josiah and his seven children created a sense of welcome at Maer that was very different from the strict atmosphere at Charles's home. The youngest child, Emma, was just a year younger than Charles and already well educated abroad and in London. Charming and messy, she was known affectionately as "Little Miss Slip-Slop" for her disorganized ways.

Charles's performance at school slipped even fur-ther, and his father was not amused. Too much fun was making Charles a dull boy, he thought. He needed to be pulled back from the brink before he became a "dis-grace" to his family.

The doctor thought he had the perfect solution. It had already been decided that twenty-one-year-old Ras would attend Edinburgh University in Scotland to study medicine. Edinburgh was the best medical school in Britain—the first Erasmus Darwin and Robert himself had also studied there. Why shouldn't sixteen-year-old Charles go with his brother to Scotland and prepare to enter the family profession?

Charles was willing. What could be better than being on his own in a new, unexplored town? In the fall of 1825, he and Ras rented a room and settled in. Determined to make a go of it, Charles dove into his books. But he soon realized that everything about the field of medicine repulsed him.

He dreaded the anatomy lectures. His professor often showed up straight from the operating room, covered with blood and filth. The dissecting theaters themselves were beyond disgusting, where limbs and organs from the corpses were piled on tables. Charles was so horrified that he never learned correct dissection techniques.

And he found the operations on live human patients to be unbearable. In those days, before anesthetics or effective pain-killing medications, patients were strapped down and operated on while they were still awake. Doctors cut quickly to reduce the stress, but patients often died on the operating table anyway. Charles, who hated the sight of blood, was horrified by

11

what he saw and could never get used to the agony of the patients. The last straw came when he had to watch an operation on a screaming child. Charles bolted out of the operating room and never returned.

Dr. Darwin was dismayed by his son's lack of ambition. "If you do not discontinue your present indulgent way, your course of study will be utterly useless," he warned sternly. But Charles couldn't summon any enthusiasm for his classes. After one year in Edinburgh, he wanted nothing to do with medicine.

Nevertheless, he returned to the university for a second year. By now he had given up almost all pretense of studying. There was plenty to occupy his time and mind, however. Taxidermy, for instance, fascinated him. As an enthusiastic hunter, Charles thought it would be valuable to learn to skin and stuff his kill. (In just one week at Maer over the summer, he had shot fifty-five partridges, three hares, and a rabbit.) He found an able taxidermist in a freed black slave named John Edmonstone, who mixed stories of his life in South America with his taxidermy lessons. The tales gave Darwin a new window into the horrors of slavery.

He also kept up his interest in natural history. His new mentor, Professor Robert Grant, was an expert on simple, tiny marine animals. With Grant, Darwin spent hours standing in frigid tidal pools scooping up primitive organisms like sponges, sea mats, and sea pens. In the spring, Darwin proudly delivered his first scientific talk at Edinburgh's Plinian Society. The waving fibers on sea mat larvae were actually microscopic hairs called cilia, he announced. They showed that the larvae could swim, which helped prove that the sedentary sea mats were indeed animals and not plants. Darwin was learning that all generalizations about animals had to be backed up by detailed, time-consuming observations of their physical structure and habits.

Another high point of his second year in Edinburgh was studying geology with Professor Robert Jameson. Geology was a hot topic in the 1820s. All over the country, geologists were discovering fossils of long-extinct plants and creatures in layers of rock. They were questioning older theories about the formation of the earth and the extinction of species.

Both Jameson and Grant were well-respected members of the scientific community. Even though he was only nineteen years old, Darwin was being taught by some of the top scientists in the world.

Rocks, sponges, sea mats—what did these have to do with medical school? Nothing, and Darwin knew it. If he wasn't going to become a doctor, he would have to find another way to earn a living. As he headed back home in the spring of 1827, one question remained on his mind.

What would he do with his life?

CHAPTER TWO
New Horizons

As always, Dr. Darwin had the answer. If Charles did not have what it took to be a doctor, perhaps he could take refuge in another respectable profession—the ministry, for instance. Many younger sons of wealthy men (the eldest son usually inherited the family estate) found lifelong employment by becoming clergymen in rural parishes.

Dr. Darwin suggested that Charles might like to become a country person.

Charles had to admit it might not be a bad idea. Many parsons, he knew, were amateur naturalists, spending as much time poring over their butterfly collections as writing their Sunday sermons. Besides, living in the country would also give him ample time to pursue his other passion, hunting.

"I'll do it," Charles agreed. So in the fall of 1827, he again took up his hated Greek and Latin textbooks, cramming for all he was worth. Right after Christmas he left for Cambridge University, where he would study theology at Christ's College.

Cambridge, one of the two most famous universities in Britain (the other was Oxford), held a host of attractions for a young man. Yes, he had to attend his tutorials in the classics, mathematics, and the Bible. But he could choose from plenty of other activities, such as playing cricket or debating or rowing on the River Cam. Of course, Charles chose to join the naturalist set, a group of youths who gathered on Friday evenings at the home of the Reverend John Stevens Henslow, a professor of botany. There they could talk about their common passion—collecting beetles!

Yes, beetling was the new craze at Cambridge in 1828. Beetles are one of the most numerous insects on earth, with about 350,000 species, and the riverbank was full of them. For many students, beetling became a competitive sport. They gathered the insects like baseball cards. "How many specimens do you have?" collectors would ask each other. "Have you found any rare species?" With the trusty guide called *An Introduction to Entomology* in one hand and a sweeping net in the other, the enthusiast waged war on beetles for miles around. Each beetle was pinned to a sheet of cardboard, properly labeled, and displayed for all to see. It was especially exciting to find a new species.

Charles bought a dog and a net, and he spent hours in the nearby fens—water-covered lowlands—with his cousin William Darwin Fox. "No pursuit at Cambridge was followed with nearly so much eagerness or gave me so much pleasure as collecting beetles," he later wrote in his autobiography.

One day he found two rare beetles by stripping bark from a tree trunk. With one beetle in each hand, he spotted a third, more valuable than the other two. Without thinking he popped one in his mouth for safekeeping and reached out to grab the third.

To his horror the one in his mouth turned out to be a type of bombardier beetle. It defended itself by spitting a stinking, burning liquid into his throat! Choking, Charles spat out the beetle, and ended up losing all three specimens.

At this point, Charles's study of theology was nearly forgotten. Once again, he had lost direction. For a while he drifted further and further away from his studies. "I have been in such a perfect & absolute state of idleness," he wrote his cousin, "that it is enough to paralyze all one's faculties; riding & walking in the morning, gambling at Van John to the most disgusting extent in the evenings…. Lord help me…."

With a great effort he pulled himself together to study for his second-year examination. To his relief and amazement, he passed. The next term, a botany course with John Stevens Henslow had him enraptured. He and the professor became good friends.

Like Darwin, Henslow was born into an upper-middle-class family and had studied to be a minister before diving into science, his real passion. Working as the curate of a small nearby church and a professor of botany at the university, he managed to support his family while pursuing his own interests. Henslow became not only Darwin's mentor, but also his role model and walking companion. People referred to Darwin as "the man who walks with Henslow."

Darwin would go to any lengths to impress his new friend. While exploring one day out in the marshy lowlands, he spied a rare insect-eating plant called a bladderwort on the other side of a pond. He thrust his pole into the boggy ground and tried to vault to the nearby bank. But the pole stuck in the mud. Darwin clutched the top for a perilous second, and then fell into the brackish water. Not discouraged, he splashed over to the bank and yanked up the bladderwort. Holding it triumphantly aloft, he waded back to the boat. Henslow was delighted.

The year sped by and the time came for Darwin's final examination. To his great joy and relief, he not only passed, but graduated tenth among 178 students. Next, he knew, would be ordination into the ministry, and then a country parish where he could attend to his church duties, study beetles, and write articles for the journal of the Royal Society.

It all sounded very respectable—and somewhat dull.

Before he buried himself forever in some country town, though, Darwin felt that he needed to shake the dust of England from his feet and see the world—at least part of the world. Perhaps he would start with the tropical Canary Islands off Africa. Dreaming wildly, he began to plan a trip to the islands, but discovered that all expeditions scheduled for that year had already set sail.

Instead, he was invited for a rock-climbing expedition in Wales. At the suggestion of Henslow, Darwin spent a week with Adam Sedgwick, the most famous geology professor at Cambridge, learning how to identify rock strata and digging for prehistoric mammal bones.

When he returned from Wales in August 1831, a letter was waiting for him—one that would change his life. As he wrote in his autobiography, "On returning home from my short geological tour in North Wales, I found a letter from Henslow, informing me that Captain FitzRoy was willing to give up part of his own cabin to any young man who would volunteer to go with him as naturalist to the Voyage of the *Beagle*."

After his father finally agreed, a very happy Charles took the express coach to Cambridge to consult with Professor Henslow. His friend informed him that another young man was also being considered for the post and that he had better persuade Captain FitzRoy in person. So on September 5, Darwin traveled to London to meet the person who held his destiny in his hands.

The two young men could not have been more different. Darwin, who was upper-middle class and politically liberal, hailed from an old Whig family that championed free thought, scientific learning, and the abolition of slavery in the British colonies. FitzRoy, by contrast, was every inch a conservative aristocrat—a descendant of King Charles II—and aware of his superior status in the world. Inflexible by upbringing, he could also be brave, resourceful, and occasionally generous. And, as Darwin was later to learn, he had a fiery temper.

New Horizons

Although just twenty-six, FitzRoy was already a seasoned commander. Three years earlier, while he was first lieutenant on HMS *Beagle,* the captain of the ship had shot himself in a fit of desperation. FitzRoy had assumed control and steered the ship home from the extreme tip of South America. This was where the *Beagle* would also be heading on its second voyage.

For this long, arduous journey in cramped quarters, FitzRoy wanted to make sure that he had a companion he liked and could talk to on equal terms. Because of the strict naval hierarchy, he could not eat with his subordinates. Only a "gentleman" could share the captain's table.

At first FitzRoy took a dislike to Darwin's blunt pug nose, perhaps because it differed so much from his own long, aristocratic one. He held the common belief that one could read a man's character by examining his facial features. As Charles told his sister, "he doubted whether anyone with my nose could possess sufficient energy and determination for the voyage."

But it wasn't long before the younger man's eagerness and intelligence won the captain over. "I like what I see of him much," FitzRoy declared enthusiastically.

Darwin, for his part, was convinced that FitzRoy was the "beau ideal of a captain." He gushed to his sister Susan, "It is no use attempting to praise him as much

as I feel inclined to do, for you would not believe me."
FitzRoy assured the inexperienced landlubber that during stormy weather, he could remain on shore for a month or two at a time, or even quit the voyage altogether if life aboard ship did not agree with him. Though such reassurances comforted his family, inwardly Darwin was determined not to give in to terror or seasickness. No matter what, he decided, he would prove himself worthy of the captain's confidence in him.

As soon as he was officially accepted as part of the expedition, Charles threw himself into a frenzy of preparation. It was already September, and FitzRoy planned to set sail by November. Not only personal items but also scientific equipment needed to be assembled and packed. Charles sent his sisters detailed instructions for the servants at The Mount. "Tell Nancy to make me soon 12 instead of 8 shirts," he wrote his sister Susan. "Tell Edward to send me up in my carpet-bag (he can slip the key in the bag tied to some string) my slippers, a pair of lightish walking-shoes—my Spanish books, my new microscope (about six inches long and 3 or four deep) which must have cotton stuffed inside; my geological compass, my Father knows [where to find] that; a little book, if I have got it in my bedroom—*Taxidermy*."

New Horizons

It was Robert Darwin, in fact, who would be generously paying for Charles's adventure, not only for food and accommodations aboard the *Beagle*, but for equipment as well. Charles decided that he must have a rifle and pistols for shooting game, or even for protection (in case they had to fight off cannibals, he thought). After consulting with experts, he packed boxes of instruments such as a compass, barometer, and telescope. He also took lobster pots, an oyster trawl for collecting marine life, a portable dissecting microscope, chemicals for experiments, and jars of alcohol to preserve animal specimens. From various ports of call along the route, Charles planned to ship boxes of specimens to Henslow back in England. The two spent a long time deciding how to store delicate jars and fossils securely so they would not be damaged during shipment.

As a parting gift, Henslow gave Charles a set of Humboldt's *Personal narrative of travels to the equinoctial regions of the new continent*. The book was inscribed with these words: "J. S. Henslow to his friend C. Darwin on his departure from England upon a voyage round the World, 21 Sept. 1831." Darwin also made room for other books—Milton's epic poem *Paradise Lost*, the Bible, the first volume of Charles Lyell's new book on geology—in his bags and boxes.

In early September, Charles took time out from packing to attend the impressive coronation procession of King William IV in London. A few days later, he and FitzRoy set off to the port city of Plymouth to view the *Beagle* for the first time.

When they arrived at the docks, Darwin felt his heart sink. The *Beagle* looked like a complete wreck. She was undergoing extensive repairs, and workers had stripped her of masts and bulkheads. Darwin knew that all the improvements would make her a more seaworthy ship, but in the meantime she was disturbingly skeletal.

She was also really small: only 90 feet long and 24 1/2 feet wide. In this limited space, seventy-four people would be crammed. FitzRoy told Darwin that he would live and sleep in the poop cabin, a 10- by 11-foot space in the stern of the ship. During the day, he would share the cabin and huge chart table with the assistant surveyor and midshipman. At night, he would sleep alone in a hammock slung above the table. A built-in set of drawers along one wall would house all his scientific paraphernalia. "The absolute want of room is an evil that nothing can surmount," Darwin later complained to Henslow.

Considering the space available, though, FitzRoy had done everything possible to make his shipmate feel comfortable. Darwin tried hard to think of the cabin as cozy, and not claustrophobic.

Just before he left Plymouth, he saw his brass name-plate fitted above the cabin door. Now he was officially a part of the expedition.

Darwin met the officers and crew, whom he found a "very intelligent, active, determined set of young fellows." Over the next five years, Darwin would get to know them very well. Among them were the first lieutenant, John Wickham; second lieutenant James Sulivan; fourteen-year-old midshipman, Philip Gridley King; nineteen-year-old assistant surveyor, John Lort Stokes; and the surgeon, Robert McCormick. In this age before photography, the captain had also hired Augustus Earle as the resident artist to portray all the exotic places the ship would visit.

In addition, there would be three native South American passengers, Fuegians from Tierra del Fuego at the tip of the continent. FitzRoy had picked them up on his previous trip to South America, and he had decided to take them back to England for a religious education. On this voyage, he planned to return them, together with an English missionary, to their own people.

FitzRoy took this opportunity to explain to Darwin in more detail the mission of the expedition. The

British Admiralty needed accurate charts so merchant ships could safely navigate the South American coast-line when they came to trade goods from England. The Admiralty had charged the *Beagle* with surveying the coast—the shores of Brazil, Argentina, Chile, and Peru—and then with sailing westward across the Pacific, to accurately measure the longitude of the world.

After saying his goodbyes at home, Charles returned to Plymouth and was ready to sail by October 24. To his disappointment, he found carpenters still busy making the ship ready for the voyage. Impatient to depart, Charles whiled away the time with social engagements and nautical study.

On December 4, he slept aboard for the first time. "I intend sleeping in my hammock. I did so last night & experienced a most ludicrous difficulty in getting into it; my great fault of jockeying was in trying to put my legs in first. The hammock being suspended, I thus only succeeded in pushing it away without making any progress in inserting my own body. The correct method is to sit accurately in centre of bed, then give yourself a dexterous twist & your head & feet come into their respective places. After a little time I daresay I shall, like others, find it very comfortable."

The only way the whole length of his body would fit, he discovered, was if he pulled out a drawer and stuck his feet in it.

The next morning he awoke expecting to set sail, but a sudden storm dashed his hopes. Twice the *Beagle* actually left Plymouth, only to be forced back into the safety of the harbor by heavy gales. Finally, on December 27, a friendly breeze from the east filled the sails and the *Beagle* glided forth into the Atlantic.

Charles Darwin's great adventure had begun.

CHAPTER THREE
Distant Shores
December 27, 1831–July 4, 1832

Charles had never dreamed he could feel so awful. The *Beagle* pitched up and down on the heavy seas of the cold North Atlantic. With every roll of the ship, Darwin's stomach gave a heave. He was deathly ill. "The misery I endured from sea-sickness is far beyond what I ever guessed at," he wrote his family.

To make matters worse, the poop cabin where Darwin worked and slept was in the stern, the rear of the ship. There the lurching never stopped. As his hammock swung back and forth, back and forth, he had "dark and gloomy thoughts." Why, oh why, had he ever left dry land?

The brutal side of naval life came as another shock. As soon as they were at sea, Captain FitzRoy had four men flogged for being drunk and disobedient. Among them, they received 134 lashes from a cat-o'-nine-tails.

The sailors' screams as the whip ripped open their backs only made Darwin feel sicker.

Yet as the *Beagle* sailed south, the winds calmed down and the air grew warmer. Darwin's spirits began to improve. Gradually he settled into the routine of life aboard ship.

Breakfast was served at 8:00 a.m. in the captain's cabin. Then Darwin settled in for four hours of work: dissecting and cataloging animal specimens, reading, writing, and thinking. When the weather was rough, Charles would lie across the huge chart table until his stomach calmed down. Then he got back to his studies.

Dinner, usually a simple meal of rice, peas, and bread, was at 1:00 p.m. Supper, at 5:00, included meat and fruits like apples and lemons to ward off scurvy. "I find a ship a very comfortable house," he wrote his father, "with everything you want, and if it was not for sea-sickness, the whole world would be sailors."

After almost a month at sea, the ship anchored in the harbor of one of the Cape Verde Islands, off the coast of western Africa. Darwin stepped onto solid land with relief. Hiking over the black volcanic rock, he marveled at the sights—gnarled baobab trees, wild cats, brilliant kingfishers. He poked among the rocks at low tide and spied an octopus hiding in its den. He gave it a jab, and it shot across the pool, spraying black ink in its wake.

At the slightest contact, it would transform from red to brown to yellowish green.

The new sights of this fascinating land were so astonishing, he wrote, that it was "like giving to a blind man eyes."

In the harbor Charles was startled to see a band of white rock running horizontally along the sea cliff. When he examined the band, he discovered it was made up of crushed seashells and corals. He knew that these shells, now 45 feet above sea level, had once been under water. But what force, he wondered, had thrust the land up out of the ocean?

It was a question many young scientists were asking. In 1832, geology was in the midst of a revolution. For thousands of years, most people had accepted literally the biblical view of the creation of the earth. But in the early 1800s, scientists began to study the strata, or rock layers, in the earth. They discovered that the lowest and oldest strata held fossils of organisms that no longer existed on earth. A French anatomist named Georges Cuvier proposed that such plants and animals had become extinct because of sudden, catastrophic geological changes. A volcano, for instance, might have suddenly created a whole new island. A great flood might have wiped out a whole species of animal.

However, more recent scientific discoveries were

calling the catastrophic view of creation and extinction into question. Changes in the earth had definitely occurred. But were those changes sudden and violent? Or were they gradual and continual?

In 1830, Charles Lyell's controversial new book, *The Principles of Geology*, had boldly attempted to answer these questions. Darwin was well acquainted with this important work. Lyell argued that the earth was in a constant state of change, as a result of the planet's movements as well as pressure, climate changes, and volcanic activity. To Darwin, the white line in the cliff seemed to support Lyell's argument. When he inspected it, he could see that the line was smooth and regular, as if the island had slowly risen out of the sea. If it had shot up suddenly and violently, he surmised, the white line would have been jagged. Darwin's observations on the island reinforced his confidence in Lyell's theory. The whole world was slowly and gradually changing.

The *Beagle* sped south, toward the equator. Seasoned sailors warned Darwin that a special ceremony awaited those who "crossed the line" for the first time. Sure enough, as soon as the ship rode into the Southern Hemisphere on February 16, the festivities began. Darwin waited belowdecks with the other new sailors for his name to be called. "Darwin, look up here!" the voice of the captain boomed out.

Cautiously Darwin climbed the ladder to the foredeck and peered over. What a strange sight met his eyes! Father Neptune, with a crown on his head and a trident in his hand, was seated on a throne in the middle of the deck. Around him danced shrieking, half-naked demons, painted in garish reds and yellows.

With a yelp of surprise, Darwin turned and fled down the ladder. But he was caught, blindfolded, and taken back up on deck. The "demons" tossed him into a sail filled with salt water. They lathered his face with paint and tar and scraped some of it off with a piece of roughened iron hoop. Then they turned poor Charles upside down and dunked him in the water again.

His sea baptism was complete. Landlubber Darwin was now an "old salt."

Thirteen days later the ship made landfall in Bahia, Brazil. Darwin's first view of the tropics was magical. Years later, he was still in raptures over the "elegance of the grasses, the novelty of the parasitical plants, the beauty of the flowers, the glossy green of the foliage." He spent his first hours in a kind of daze, overwhelmed by the teeming life around him. "To a person fond of natural history," he admitted, "such a day as this brings with it a deeper pleasure than he can ever hope to experience again."

Yet one persistent evil marred this earthly paradise—slavery. In Brazil, the whole economy depended on the labor of imported African slaves. (Slavery would not be abolished in Brazil until 1888.) The Darwins and the Wedgwoods had been at the forefront of the anti-slavery movement in Britain in the early nineteenth century, when the slave trade in British colonies was abolished. Now, for the first time, Charles witnessed slavery firsthand. And what he saw appalled him.

Everywhere he looked in Brazil, black people were worked like farm animals. From dawn to dusk, they heaved and hauled, plowed, planted, and harvested. For even minor mistakes, they were punished brutally, sometimes with fatal results.

One small incident struck Darwin as particularly telling. One day while crossing a river, he tried to make himself understood in broken Spanish to a black ferryman. Using hand signals, he inadvertently waved his hand near the slave's face. Assuming that this foreigner was angry, the man immediately held up his face to be struck. "I shall never forget my feelings of surprise, disgust, and shame, at seeing a great powerful man afraid even to ward off a blow," Darwin remembered years later. "This man had been trained to a degradation lower than the slavery of the most helpless animal."

Darwin's strong views on the evils of slavery sparked one of his worst arguments with Captain FitzRoy. As a conservative and traditionalist, FitzRoy thought that slavery was inevitable. After all, he declared, it was a very old institution, dating back to biblical times. Even Abraham and Moses had owned slaves.

While they were in Bahia, FitzRoy mentioned to Darwin that he had just visited a wealthy slave owner. The man had told him that he had brought many of his slaves together and asked them whether they wished to be free. "No!" they all answered in unison.

What other answer could they give? Darwin wanted to know. The slaves were standing right in front of their master!

FitzRoy was furious at Charles's sarcastic tone. If he doubted his word, FitzRoy snapped, then he could leave his cabin immediately.

Darwin hurried out of the captain's cabin. Almost immediately, he was sorry for their spat. What if he had to leave the ship for good? When word of the quarrel spread, the other officers invited Darwin to eat in the gun room with them. But FitzRoy already regretted his hasty temper. He sent First Lieutenant Wickham to Darwin to convey his apologies. Darwin accepted.

Privately, FitzRoy actually felt pity for slaves and other oppressed people. In fact, by the end of the voyage, he had come to hate slavery almost as much as Darwin did.

The *Beagle* continued down the Brazilian coast, reaching the port city of Río de Janeiro on April 3. Darwin immediately joined a party of Englishmen riding to a coffee plantation about a hundred miles into the interior. The journey was difficult. The travelers had to contend with blazing heat, poor accommodations, and vampire bats that regularly bit and infected their horses. Yet to Darwin, the beauty of the landscape made up for any hardship.

He marveled at the abundance of plant and animal life in the jungle. Slender cabbage palm trees towered fifty feet overhead, draped with long vines called lianas and interspersed with bright green tree ferns and mimosa trees. Brilliant butterflies and hummingbirds darted from flower to flower. During the day, the cries of howler monkeys echoed for miles. At night, frogs and cicadas filled the air with song. The forest cathedral inspired Charles with feelings of "wonder, astonishment, and devotion."

As the group pushed on into the interior, they passed

a massive granite ridge. The hill was haunted, the guide told the Englishmen. Just a few years before, it had been inhabited by runaway slaves who built a little village of grass huts at the summit. Eventually, the guide explained, "they were discovered and a group of Brazilian soldiers raided the village and recaptured the runaways. Only one old woman escaped. Rather than return to slavery, she threw herself off the hill onto the rocks below.

"I was told before leaving England," Darwin wrote his sister Caroline, "that after living in slave countries all my opinions would be altered; the only alteration I am aware of is forming a much higher estimate of the Negro character."

Five days later the group reached the hacienda of Senhor Manuel Figuireda, the uncle of one of Darwin's fellow travelers. The main house, slave huts, store-houses, and stables were aligned in a kind of rectangle, with heaps of coffee beans drying in the center court-yard. As a bell announced their arrival, the small community turned out to greet the travelers. Darwin was relieved to see that, on this plantation at least, the slaves seemed well treated and relatively content.

Finally Darwin and his companions arrived at their destination, the coffee plantation of an Irishman named Patrick Lennon. Here an incident occurred that confirmed Darwin's worst impressions of slavery. Lennon suddenly began to quarrel with the plantation manager. He threatened to sell at public auction a boy the manager was fond of. Not only that, Lennon fumed, but he would break up all the families and sell the women and children too!

The whole plantation fell into an uproar. Finally Senhor Figuireda calmed Lennon down and prevented a tragedy.

Darwin believed that "the inhumanity of separating thirty families, who had lived together for many years, did not even occur to the owner." Earlier he had considered Lennon to be a decent, reasonable person. Greed, he decided, made men into monsters.

When the group returned to Río, Darwin was delighted to discover that he had two more months to explore the country while the *Beagle* returned to Bahia to continue surveying the coastline. He made good use of his time, collecting specimens one day and writing up his notes the next.

He found that the constant beauty masked an ever-present peril. All species seemed to be engaged in a constant struggle for survival. It was eat—or be eaten. One day, Charles was amazed to see hordes of panicked spiders, insects, and lizards scurrying along the forest floor. He turned to see a line of black army ants steadily advancing. At an invisible signal, the ants separated and surrounded their prey—and killed them.

Darwin studied the mud dauber wasp, which builds little mud cells for its larvae and then stuffs paralyzed spiders and caterpillars into the cells. When the young wasps hatch, their first meal is waiting for them. They devour the spiders and caterpillars alive.

Darwin was also fascinated by the many and varied species of spiders. One day he watched a battle between a wasp and spider after which the victorious wasp began dragging the body of the spider off to its nest. Darwin snatched up both victor and victim for his collection.

"I am at present red-hot with Spiders," Darwin wrote Henslow enthusiastically, "and if I am not mistaken I have already taken some new genera.... I shall have a large box to send very soon to Cambridge."

By the beginning of July, the *Beagle* was ready to venture further down the coast, to the barren, inhospitable lands of Tierra del Fuego. "I long," Darwin wrote in his journal, "to set foot where no man has trod before."

CHAPTER FOUR

To the Ends of the Earth
July 1832–February 1833

July is the middle of winter in South America, and the temperature plunged as the *Beagle* moved further south. Like the seamen, Charles Darwin grew a beard to help keep himself warm. When the wind whipped the waves into white peaks, his seasickness returned. He spent a lot of time in his hammock, reading a much-thumbed edition of Milton's *Paradise Lost*. But he was not too sick to take notes on a pod of pilot whales and "a wonderful shoal of Porpoises" that playfully leapt in front of the ship. Penguins swimming nearby bayed so loudly that the sailors thought they were mooing cattle.

One night during a storm, St. Elmo's fire lit up the masts, glowing in electric blues and greens. "Everything is in flames," Darwin wrote Henslow, "the sky with lightning, the water with luminous particles, and even the very masts are pointed with a blue flame."

Twenty-eight days out of Río, they neared the port of Buenos Aires, Argentina, on the south bank of the Río Plata. As they headed to anchor, an Argentinean guard ship fired a blank warning shot over their bow. The *Beagle* kept going. The guard ship fired another round, this time with live bullets that whistled through the rigging. Captain FitzRoy was furious. What fool would dare fire on a British vessel? He anchored the ship and promptly dispatched two boats to shore. The British consul would hear about this insult to the British flag!

Darwin rowed with the others toward the dock. Before they could land, an Argentinean customs boat intercepted them. "Return to your ship!" the customs officer barked. "You are under quarantine!" Apparently the health inspector was worried about English ships bringing in cholera, a terrible contagious disease, even though the *Beagle* had been at sea for seven months.

FitzRoy was fuming when Darwin and the others returned. He fired off a complaint of uncivil treatment to both the governor of Buenos Aires and the British Admiralty. Then he readied his guns and skimmed past the guard ship. "If you fire on us again, I'll send a broadside into your rotten hulk!" he roared.

To the Ends of the Earth

With that, the captain set the course for Montevideo, a Uruguayan town on the north side of the river. It was like going from the frying pan into the fire. As soon as they moored, the minister of the military government requested an audience with FitzRoy. His troops were rebelling, he announced to the captain. Could the *Beagle* send military reinforcements?

The crew of the *Beagle* came ashore ready to storm the central fort. They were "heavily armed with Muskets, Cutlasses, and Pistols," Darwin wrote in his journal. Darwin marched down the main street with the others, pistol and sword drawn. He was prepared to fight—but the rebel threat melted away. The makeshift militia from the *Beagle* took control of the fort without resistance. They stayed just one night, cooked beefsteaks in the courtyard, and returned to the ship.

In the end, the rebellion petered out and no one was hurt. Yet Darwin enjoyed the thrill of near battle. "There is certainly a great deal of pleasure in the excitement of this sort of work," he concluded. It would not be the last time that the crew of the *Beagle* was swept up in the tumult of South American politics.

They pressed on to the main mission of the voyage: charting the unmapped coastline of Patagonia, the long tail of South America. They dropped anchor off Bahia

Blanca, a rough frontier settlement filled with Indians, European adventurers, and Argentinean gauchos. These skilled cowboys were a rough-and-ready bunch, with their long mustaches, huge knives, and tough, swift horses. Darwin got to know the gauchos well during the next few years. Quick to quarrel but always polite, they looked "as if they would cut your throat and make a bow at the same time."

Spring was now in the air. Darwin spent most of his time at one of his favorite pursuits—hunting. The flat plains of Patagonia teemed with deer, wild pigs, armadillos, ostriches, and a relative of the camel called a guanaco. These curious beasts were especially easy to fool. All Darwin had to do was lie on the ground and wave his legs in the air, and the guanaco would draw near to see what all the fuss was about. Then Darwin would jump up and shoot it.

One fascinating find was a black toad with slashes of bright crimson on its stomach and the soles of its feet. Charles saw one on a dry, dusty road and put it in a pond of water as a "treat"—only to discover that the toad couldn't swim! Hastily, he fished it out again.

His most prized discoveries in Patagonia, however, were not living animals, but the remains of long-dead ones—fossils. While cruising around the bay at Punta

Alta, Darwin spied some teeth and a thighbone sticking out of a low bank. The next day he returned with pickax and shovel and began to dig.

The bones proved to be parts of an animal as large as a rhinoceros that resembled a huge armadillo. He also found the bones of what looked like giant sloths, a huge rodent, and a grazing animal built like a hippopotamus. Altogether, Darwin reported in his book *The Voyage of the Beagle,* he found the remains of "nine great quadrapeds...embedded on the beach within the space of about 200 yards square."

Darwin was immediately struck by the fact that the extinct species looked like contemporary South American animals, but were much larger. Questions raced through his head. Why had the earlier species become extinct? How were they related to the present-day species? Had the larger species somehow changed into the smaller ones? Did this mean that living plants and animals were also in the process of continual change, like the earth?

"This wonderful relationship in the same continent between the dead and the living will, I do not doubt, hereafter throw more light on the appearance of organic beasts on Earth and their disappearance from it," Darwin concluded.

After each hard day of digging, Darwin came back to the *Beagle* and dumped the ancient bones on the deck, much to the disgust of tidy First Lieutenant Wickham, who complained loudly about the mess. Yet Charles could not contain his excitement. "I have been wonderfully lucky," he wrote home. In 1832, only one fossil of an extinct South American animal had been taken to Europe. It was a megatherium, a giant sloth, and it was on display in Madrid. When Henslow received the first box crammed with Darwin's finds, European scientists would have a treasure trove of fossils to study.

The time came to venture down to the very tip of the continent, to the no-man's-land known as Tierra del Fuego. One of the trip's purposes, dear to FitzRoy's heart, was to take his three Fuegian passengers home again. He had brought them to England to teach them Christianity and expose them to civilization. His great hope was that they could return to their own people as missionaries, to spread the gospel and demonstrate how to use tools. Originally he had taken four Fuegians from their homeland to England, but one had died from smallpox. Now there were three, all now known by the names the English had given them: York Minster, a twenty-seven-year-old man; Jemmy Button, a fifteen-year-old boy; and Fuegia Basket, a ten-year-old girl. During their year in England, they had been educated at the Church Missionary Society where they learned English language and manners.

Although the Fuegians were returning to one of the coldest, most desolate and windswept areas on earth, the idealistic Missionary Society had dressed them in clothes fit for a London drawing room. They outfitted York Minster and Jemmy Buttons in trousers, frock coats, and white kid gloves; they gave Fuegia Basket a pretty dress to wear for the journey. In addition, to help export their civilization to the wilderness the Society had packed all sorts of English knickknacks: wineglasses, a set of china, tea trays, and books.

Darwin liked the three Fuegians, especially little Fuegia Basket. Yet he was skeptical of the mission. Their country was a "broken mass of wild rocks, lofty hills, and useless forests: and these are viewed through mists and endless storms." In such a place, what could anyone possibly do with tea trays?

Nothing could have prepared Darwin for his first view of these people in their own habitat. As the *Beagle* sailed into Good Success Bay on December 17, the natives were perched on a cliff, yelling, gesticulating, and leaping up and down. The next morning, Darwin and FitzRoy went ashore with a party of sailors to meet them. "It was without doubt the most curious and interesting spectacle I ever beheld," Darwin remembered. Even in the frigid air, the Fuegians were naked, except for tattered guanaco skins thrown over their shoulders. Their hair was filthy and matted, their faces painted, and their language, to Darwin's ears, an unintelligible series of grunts and clicks. To the proper Englishman, they seemed like the "troubled spirits of another world."

They lived in the most primitive way possible, sleeping on the cold wet ground beneath animal skin tents. They did not know how to grow or harvest plants. Instead, they scavenged for seaweed and shellfish while hunting for fish, birds, and marine mammals like seals and dolphins.

The Fuegians were great mimics. When Darwin laughed, they laughed; when he coughed, they coughed. He was startled at their uncanny ability to "repeat with perfect correctness each word in any sentence we addressed them," even though they did not understand the meaning of what they were saying. Hours later, they could still imitate the sounds in the sentence.

A few days later, the crew came across another group of Fuegians, the "most abject and miserable creatures"

Darwin had ever seen. Rowing out in a canoe to greet the ship, they were absolutely naked, protected only by the grease they had smeared across their bodies. A naked woman was nursing her equally naked child. Even in the driving sleet and rain, neither was shivering. Darwin could not understand how the three cultured Fuegians he knew so well could be related to the wretched beings he saw before him.

FitzRoy was determined to deliver Jemmy Buttons, York Minster, and Fuegia Basket back to their own people. They first reached Jemmy's homeland in pleasant, fertile Ponsonby Sound. York Minster and Fuegia Basket decided to stay there, as did the missionary Richard Matthews, who longed to convert the tribe to Christianity.

The sailors immediately erected three large wigwams. They brought crates of gardening and fishing tools from the ship and began digging a garden. FitzRoy wanted to introduce agriculture to this hunting-and-gathering people so they could grow their own vegetables and grain. In addition, the Englishmen unloaded boxes containing European clothes, fine white linen, soup tureens, and mahogany dressing cases, and placed everything in the tents.

The next morning Jemmy was reunited with his mother and brothers. At first they stared at each other wordlessly. Forgetting his own language, Jemmy tried a mixture of broken English and Spanish. *"No sabe?"* ("You do not understand?") he said when his brothers did not respond. Yet despite the communication gap, everyone appeared friendly. The women were particularly nice to Fuegia Basket.

FitzRoy decided to leave the Fuegians to get reacquainted and took a few days to explore the Beagle Channel, which he had named during the previous voyage. In a scene of dramatic beauty, the small column of whaleboats drifted down the narrow waterway. Snow-white glaciers, mirrored in the crystal blue sea, rose steeply on either side. That night, the group camped close by an overhanging glacier. Suddenly, with a deep roar, a huge chunk of ice broke away and crashed into the water. A massive wave rushed down the channel!

In an instant, the boats they had pulled up onto the shore were totally swamped. Darwin thought fast. He knew that if the boats were swept away, their party would be stranded. With another sailor, he sped down the beach. As a second and then a third wave rolled over their heads, he tied the ropes more securely to the moorings. Darwin had saved the day—and he got his reward. FitzRoy was so thankful that he named the glacier Mount Darwin.

To the Ends of the Earth

After nine days, they returned to the settlement—and found chaos. As soon as the exploring party had left in the whaleboats, the Fuegians had raided the camp and looted the wigwams. All the china was broken and the fine linen ripped apart, divided among the members of the tribe. Some men had even threatened the life of poor Matthews, the missionary. York Minster and even Fuegia Basket were scared and had sided with the Fuegians. Only Jemmy was upset by the behavior of his countrymen. He apologized repeatedly.

FitzRoy was gravely disappointed and disillusioned. It would not be as simple to civilize—or Christianize—a savage people as he had hoped. He had no choice but to welcome the terrified Matthews back on board. The three Fuegians who had been to England, however, would stay where they were and try to resume a normal life among their own people. The *Beagle* would return in a year to see how they were doing.

For Darwin, the lesson was clear. It was impossible to civilize a people who did not understand the meaning of property and who had no chief to maintain law and order. He also saw that in the meantime, the Fuegian people, like the Indians of North and South America and the Aborigines of Australia, would probably be the losers in any contact with Europeans.

Darwin wished the best for York Minster, Jemmy Button, and little Fuegia Basket. But he was not optimistic about their future.

CHAPTER FIVE

Gauchos and Guanacos
March 1833–March 1834

For much of the next year, Darwin was on his own in the wilds of South America. As the *Beagle* continued to spend months out at sea, Darwin pushed into the interior of Argentina. There he would encounter not only wild animals but also brutal soldiers, ruthless cowboys, and vengeful Indians. Everywhere, the stronger dominated the weaker—and the weaker perished.

It was a dangerous time for Darwin. But it was a thrilling time, too.

The ship's first stop after Tierra del Fuego was the Falkland Islands, off the eastern shore of Argentina. To the officers' surprise, they learned that British warships had just claimed the islands for Britain. FitzRoy took the opportunity to purchase with his own money (and without permission from the Admiralty) a small American vessel that had been used for seal hunting.

He wanted another ship to help with the surveying, since the constant storms had slowed the *Beagle*'s progress.

The new ship had to be refitted, so the expedition party went north again. When they docked in the port of Maldonado, a small Uruguayan town swarming with cowboys and cattle, Darwin went ashore. He hired two guides to ride with him into open country. They were armed with pistols and sabers to guard against the ever-present bandits. With them they took twelve horses, a precaution in case one or more grew lame. More than one unwary traveler had been left stranded on the empty plains when his horse gave out on him.

Weeks of galloping across the "endless green hills" left Darwin tired, yet exhilarated. He was struck by the large numbers of novel birds and animals. Flocks of rhea, an ostrich-like bird, clustered on the hillsides, protecting nests that contained as many as twenty-seven eggs. Finding one nest meant dinner for days. Plump capybaras, the world's biggest rodents, lived along the edges of the many lakes.

The largest four-legged creatures Darwin met outside Maldonado were male deer. They had such a strong odor that they could be detected half a mile away. Darwin made the mistake of carrying a piece of deerskin in his pocket handkerchief. He could never get rid of the smell, no matter how many times he washed it.

The local farmers and gauchos weren't sure what to make of this strange, rock-collecting Englishman. "Being able to talk very little Spanish," he wrote, "I was looked at with much pity, wonder, & a great deal of kindness." The ranchers were unfailingly hospitable, even if all they had to offer was a mud floor, a cigar, and a little guitar music.

Back on the *Beagle*, the piles of specimens became too much for Darwin to handle alone. He counted eighty species of birds, nine kinds of snakes, and many other reptiles. Including the plants, insects, fish, fungi, and rocks, he had collected a total of 1,529 specimens. All of the animals needed to be skinned and stuffed, and everything had to be inventoried. As many specimens as possible had to be packed in jars filled with spirits of wine and packed for shipment to Henslow, back in England. Clearly, Darwin needed an assistant.

He found one in sixteen-year-old Syms Covington, described on the crew list as a fiddler and errand boy for the poop cabin. Covington turned out to be very helpful. Eventually he took over most of the shooting and collecting duties, and even learned to catalog his finds. Covington would stay with Darwin for many years after they returned to England.

By now Charles was eager to sail around the tip of South America and see Chile and the great Andes Mountains on the Pacific coast. But FitzRoy had not yet completed his survey of the Atlantic coast. So when the *Beagle*, accompanied by the smaller ship, which had been renamed HMS *Adventure*, sailed south toward the Río Negro, Darwin hit on a daring plan. He would take advantage of the *Beagle*'s absence to explore the 500 miles of grassy plains between the Río Negro in the south and the Río Plata in the north. The pampas, as the vast grassland region was known, was an uninvestigated treasure house of geological marvels and exotic plants and animals.

It was also an extremely dangerous area, inhabited by roving bands of Indians. A few generations earlier, the native Pampas Indians had lived in villages of two or three thousand people each. But white settlers and their diseases had destroyed most of the population. Even though the Indians were excellent horsemen and fierce fighters, their days seemed to be numbered.

To make the region safe for cattle ranching, the Argentinean government was determined to wipe out whatever Indians still remained. It had dispatched an army led by the ruthless general Juan Manuel de Rosas with orders to "exterminate the Indian." The general now controlled the pampas, so Darwin would need a signed pass from him if he wanted to explore the area.

The *Beagle* dropped Darwin off at the town of El Carmen de Patagones on the Río Negro. He arranged with FitzRoy to rendezvous at Bahia Blanca, 500 miles to the north. Then, with six gauchos and a British trader, Darwin set off for General Rosas's camp on the Río Colorado. After two days the party arrived at the rough-and-tumble headquarters. Darwin knew that Rosas was an immensely wealthy rancher, popular with his men and merciless to the Indians. But he wasn't sure what to expect from the interview.

He needn't have worried. Rosas was a "perfect gaucho" himself, dressed in a colorful poncho and fringed riding pants. Darwin came away with a passport, a pledge for government horses, and a positive opinion of the most feared soldier in Argentina. Years later, though, this seemingly polite man would become a tyrannical dictator.

On August 16, Darwin and his guides struck out into open country. He reveled in the "independence of the Gaucho life, to be able at any moment to pull up your horse and say here we will pass the night." They rode hard all day, hunting for game, and at night they slept under the stars. Like a true gaucho, the English country gentleman learned to live on a diet of nothing but meat, varied by an occasional ostrich egg. The gauchos taught Darwin how to rope the legs of an ostrich with a *bola*, a lasso with two heavy metal balls on the ends. The ostriches tasted a lot like beef, Darwin discovered. Armadillos, cooked in their shells, tasted more like duck.

He took detailed notes on every animal he saw. The shy, quick armadillos, he wrote, were almost impossible to catch because they burrowed down into the sand seconds after sensing danger. As soon as Darwin caught sight of one, he would dive off his saddle and try to grab it. But he was never quick enough.

A small, mole-like rodent called the tuco-tuco also made a strong impression on Darwin. When he lay on the ground to sleep, the creatures kept up an incessant grunting from their underground lair all night long.

He never tired of seeing the flocks of rhea rising all together into the air, startled by the thunder of horses' hooves. From the gauchos he heard about a rare species of rhea that was smaller and darker than its cousins. He hoped to sight one, but it proved quite elusive.

When they arrived at the settlement of Bahia Blanca,

there was no *Beagle* in sight. Too restless to sit around and wait, Charles bought a horse and rode up to Punta Alta with a few other men in hopes of finding more fossils. Sure enough, he dug up a nearly entire horse-sized skeleton with a long narrow snout. It was, he decided, some sort of prehistoric sloth.

"There is nothing like geology," he wrote gleefully to his sister Catherine. "The pleasure of the first day's partridge shooting or the first day's hunting cannot be compared to finding a fine group of fossil bones, which tell the story of former times with almost a living tongue."

Rumors of Indian wars kept following them. One day came news that five men at a nearby military outpost had been murdered. The 300 soldiers who were sent in pursuit of the murderers stayed overnight at Darwin's camp. Nothing Darwin had ever seen was so "wild and savage." The soldiers slaughtered cattle for their supper and then, being drunk, proceeded to drink the animals' blood. They never ran down their quarry, who escaped into the wilds of the pampas and were not heard from again.

One Spaniard told Darwin about another recent expedition launched against an Indian tribe. Two hundred of General Rosas's men had tracked them down by the dust raised by their horses' hoofs. Then they descended upon the terrified group, killing all the adults and kidnapping the children to be sold into slavery.

Most shocking to Darwin was learning that the soldiers were slaughtering all Indian women over the age of twenty "in cold blood." He protested to the Spaniard that such treatment was inhuman.

It was necessary, came the matter-of-fact answer. He told Darwin that the women had too many children. And, after all, he added, the orders from the Argentinean government were to "exterminate all the Indians."

"Who would believe in this age that such atrocities could be committed in a Christian, civilized country?" Darwin wrote in his diary. Clearly the "white Gaucho savages" who ran the nation were "inferior in every moral virtue."

On August 4, the *Beagle* had dropped anchor at Bahia Blanca, only to depart shortly for another surveying trip. So Darwin set out on the second leg of his great overland expedition, 400 miles northward to Buenos Aires. Accompanied by only two guides, he traveled from one rude military outpost to another. They took shelter in tiny hovels made of thistle stalks and ate only what they caught each day—ostrich, armadillo, deer.

Gauchos and Guanacos

Darwin climbed mountains, crossed rivers, and witnessed a hailstorm with hailstones as big as apples. At one campfire he was astonished to find that the veal-like meat he was enjoying was actually that of an unborn puma. It was quite a delicacy, he was told.

The English country gentleman who had first boarded the *Beagle* two years before had been transformed. Gone was the dandy with long trousers, shiny boots, and spotless waistcoat. In his place stood a rugged, sunburned gaucho, with long beard, dusty leggings, and wide-brimmed hat. He was no longer merely Charles Darwin. He had been reborn, as his passport from General Rosas read, as *el Naturalista* Don Carlos.

Buenos Aires, he found when he reached it, was a large port city with wide, straight boulevards. He took note of the many beautiful young women wrapped in lacy black shawls. Their dark eyes did not hold his attention long, though. Within seven days he was off again on an excursion to Santa Fé, 300 miles to the northwest.

Of the many unusual animals in the region he was particularly fascinated by the viscacha, which looked like a large rabbit with a long tail. In front of every viscacha burrow, Darwin noted, rose a mound of "cattle bones, stones, thistle-stalks, hard lumps of earth, dry dung, etc." Apparently the viscacha had dragged all these treasures home itself. But why? No one knew. "No doubt there must exist some good reason," Darwin thought. But he couldn't figure it out.

Along the Río Parana near Santa Fé, he discovered a fossil deposit containing the remains of a giant armadillo, a Toxodon, and a mastodon. Much to his surprise and delight, he discovered the tooth of an extinct horse in the same layer of rock. Darwin was well aware that when Columbus arrived in the New World in 1492, the explorer had found no native horses there. He also knew that in 1535, Spanish con-quistadors had released seven stallions and five mares near present-day Buenos Aires and that their descendants had eventually populated half of South America. Yet here was evidence that a native horse had once galloped on the pampas—and then disappeared—long before the arrival of the Europeans.

In Santa Fé, Darwin fell ill with a fever and was nursed by a local woman who wanted to try local remedies "too disgusting to mention." Rather than allow her to experiment on him, he decided to escape on a packet ship going down the Río Parana toward Buenos Aires. Once aboard, he began to feel better.

Gauchos and Guanacos

When they moored on a jungle island, Darwin got off to explore. He had gone only a few hundred yards when he saw the unmistakable tracks of a jaguar! Someone told him that he was in *el rastro del tigre,* the "track of the tiger." On every island they visited, he saw trees raked with long, deep scratches. This was where the jaguars sharpened their claws, the fearful locals explained. No it wasn't, Darwin decided. It was where they *trimmed* their claws.

When the boat reached the mouth of the river, Darwin disembarked—and was immediately seized by a body of armed soldiers. Argentina was in the middle of a revolution! Friends of General Rosas had risen up against the governor of Buenos Aires and surrounded the city. Now no one was allowed in or out of Buenos Aires or any of its ports. Darwin was stuck just where he was—a prisoner.

He was frantic. What if the *Beagle* left without him? Appeals to General Rolor, who commanded the northern rebels, got Darwin a pass to the commander in chief south of the city. Darwin and his guide galloped around Buenos Aires to the camp, where he had a polite but frustrating meeting with the commander. Luckily, General Rosas's brother was also there, and Darwin mentioned his friendly meeting with the general. Rosas's name worked like magic. Suddenly

Darwin had permission to enter Buenos Aires—but he had to go by himself, and on foot.

In the city, shops were closed and the streets empty. All the citizens seemed to be in hiding. Bands of lawless soldiers roamed everywhere. Darwin bribed an official to smuggle in his servant, Syms Covington, who was trapped at a neighboring estate where he had been bird hunting. He listened as Covington told a frightening tale about how he had nearly lost his life—and *had* lost Darwin's gun—in a bed of quicksand. After dodging bullets for two weeks, the two finally managed to squeeze onto a crowded packet to Montevideo, where the *Beagle* was waiting for them.

Darwin had spent two years exploring the east coast of South America. He was eager to move on.

Preparing to go to sea again, he packed up two boxes of "nearly 200 skins of birds and animals," fish, insects, mice, seeds, and fossils. He was nervous about sending all of these treasures to Henslow. It had been months since he'd shipped the first box, and he had not received one letter from his friend. Had Darwin's precious specimens ever arrived in England—or were they lost forever at the bottom of the sea?

On December 7, the *Beagle* and the *Adventure* weighed anchor and sailed forth into the Atlantic. Ten

miles out, they skimmed through a flock of white butterflies that stretched as far as the eye could see. The
sailors called out that it was snowing butterflies!

They headed south, where FitzRoy would take his
last measurements of the Patagonian coast. Christmas
1833 found them celebrating at Port Desire, competing in "Olympic games" and feasting on an unusual
bird shot by the ship's artist. Only after he had satisfied
his hunger did Darwin remember the stories the gauchos had told of a small, dark rhea. He had been looking for the mysterious bird for over a year—and now
he had just eaten one!

To Darwin's great relief, the head, some feathers,
and many of the bones were still left. He fished them
out of the garbage and preserved them. Four years later
he found out that his prize had been named after him:
the *Rhea darwinii*.

Now the *Beagle* had an important promise to fulfill.
When FitzRoy had left the Fuegians behind in Tierra
del Fuego, he had said he would return. In March
1834, a year later, the *Beagle* dropped anchor once
more in the little cove in Ponsonby Sound.

All was silent. From a distance, they could see that
the wigwams were deserted, the gardens flattened and
ruined. What had happened?

A canoe approached, flying a little flag. The Fuegian in it seemed to be wiping the paint off his face—it was Jemmy!

But it was not a Jemmy they recognized. This man was "thin, pale, and without a remnant of clothes, except for an old blanket." Darwin was shocked at the transformation. "We had left him plump, fat, clean and well-dressed," he wrote. "I never saw so complete and grievous a change."

Jemmy seemed in good spirits, though, and was very glad to see his old shipmates. Though he had forgotten some of his English, with a change of clothes he was fit for the captain's table. Over dinner, he told his tale.

York Minster had betrayed him. He had married Fuegia and persuaded Jemmy to accompany them to York's home island. Then, while Jemmy was sleeping, York and his friends had stolen all of his possessions and left Jemmy as naked as when FitzRoy had first found him.

FitzRoy wanted to save his friend and asked him to return to England on the *Beagle*.

No, no, Jemmy told him. He wanted to remain with his own people. He had "plenty fruits," "plenty birdies," and "too much fish." He had even built his own canoe.

Gauchos and Guanacos

Darwin soon discovered that Jemmy had an even more important reason for wanting to stay. A fine-looking young Fuegian woman paddled up in a canoe and waited alongside the ship, weeping loudly. Jemmy was married! His wife was very afraid he wouldn't return. Not until he climbed down the ladder of the ship did she stop her wailing.

As a farewell gift, Jemmy presented fine otter skins to FitzRoy and two spearheads to Darwin. In return, the officers loaded him with presents, including a shawl and a gold-laced cap for his wife. They shook hands all round with Jemmy, very sorry to say goodbye. As the ship sailed away, he lit a signal fire on shore. It was, Darwin wrote, a "last and long farewell."

CHAPTER SIX

Fire in the Earth
April 1834–September 1835

Darwin received some good news. All of his precious boxes had arrived in England!

Before heading toward the Pacific Ocean, the *Beagle* returned to the Falkland Islands to get supplies. There Darwin found a bundle of mail waiting for him—including a letter from John Henslow. Darwin and his discoveries were the talk of Britain, Henslow reported. Scientists were going crazy over his plants and animals. They were in raptures over his megatherium fossils.

"Your name is likely to be immortalized," another old friend reported grandly.

So all of his exhausting work (and months of sea-sickness) had been worth it after all. Not only was he *el Naturalista Don Carlos* to the Argentinean gauchos. He was also Charles Darwin, famous naturalist, to the important scientists at the British Association for the Advancement of Science!

Henslow told his friend to keep up the good work, and avoid becoming disheartened. "I suspect you will always find something to keep up your courage," he wrote.

Darwin needed the encouragement, because the past months had been difficult. He eagerly looked forward to rounding Cape Horn and crossing into the Pacific, whose name meant "peaceful." After what had seemed like an eternity in the cold, gray Atlantic, he longed for warm, clear skies and crystal blue water. Instead, he suffered through some of the worst storms of his journey. Howling winds and huge waves battered the small craft as HMS *Beagle* and her companion ship *Adventure* braved the icy Straits of Magellan to reach the western shore of South America. "The sight of such a coast," Darwin wrote, "is enough to make a landsman dream for a week about shipwrecks, peril, and death."

The bad weather continued as they struggled up the coast. This is an "anything but Pacific Ocean," Darwin complained. Not until they reached the charming town of Valparaiso, Chile, on July 22, 1834, did storms give way to sunshine. The clear, dry air in the harbor smelled of flowers.

Fire in the Earth

Thankful to be on land again, Darwin found lodging with an English merchant who was an old friend from Shrewsbury School. He rambled through the countryside, investigating beds of seashells lodged in the cliffs not far from Valparaiso. The cliffs, some of them rising 1,300 feet above sea level, had been beaches in the recent geological past. Surprisingly, Darwin saw relatively few insects, birds, or mammals in the area. Why would that be, he wondered, on a continent teeming with animals? Perhaps, he wrote in his diary, "the want of animals may be owing to none having been created since this country was raised from the sea." To him it was one more indication that all animals had not been created at the same time.

Darwin was most eager to explore the foothills of the Andes Mountains, which rose majestically above the town. With a guide and a troop of mules, he set off to climb Campana Mountain, 6,400 feet high. Halfway up, the visibility was so good they could spy the masts of ships in the bay of Valparaiso, twenty-six miles away. The setting sun painted the snow-covered Andes a deep ruby red. The view from the summit was even more awe-inspiring: "Chile, bounded by the Andes and the Pacific, was seen as in a map," Darwin remembered. "Who can avoid wondering at the force which has upheaved these mountains, and…at the countless ages which it must have required to have broken through, removed, and levelled whole masses of them?"

Darwin explored Chile for six weeks altogether, dining with English merchants in the capital city of Santiago and visiting the gold mines of San Fernando. There each of the miners lugged 200 pounds of stone out of the mine a day and had to survive on a diet of boiled beans and bread. Bravely, Darwin crossed wobbly bridges made of hide and sticks suspended above deep rocky ravines.

Unfortunately, his enjoyment was cut short by a bout of illness, which may have been typhoid fever. He rushed back to Valparaiso at the end of September, only to remain in bed for the next month.

In his absence, a storm had been brewing on the *Beagle*. Captain FitzRoy had been laboring around the clock for months, trying to complete the surveys he had made of the Patagonian coast. The strain had made him tense and short-tempered. Matters came to a head when the Admiralty sent him a furious letter from London. How dare the captain buy a ship without their approval? Who did he think was going to pay for it? The Admiralty flatly refused to assume the costs of the

Adventure, which FitzRoy had purchased and outfitted himself. They ordered him to sell it at once.

FitzRoy sank into despair and rage. His hard work and personal sacrifice had gone unappreciated. Clearly his superiors had no faith in him, and maybe they were right. Was his survey of Tierra del Fuego as accurate as possible? Perhaps he should return to that desolate and forbidding land to try again.

Or, better yet, maybe he should just quit. His uncle Lord Castlereagh had committed suicide, he remembered. FitzRoy worried that he had inherited the family tendency to depression. Just to be on the safe side, perhaps someone else should take charge—First Lieutenant Wickham, for instance.

In desperation, FitzRoy resigned.

The news plunged the entire crew into confusion. Without FitzRoy, Darwin feared that Wickham would give up the mission and simply take the ship back to England. There would be no voyage across the Pacific, no circling of the globe. Darwin didn't know what to do. Would all his grand plans for the voyage come to a sudden end?

"One whole night I tried to think over the pleasure of seeing Shrewsbury again," he recalled, "but the barren plains of Peru gained the day." He decided to remain and explore the rest of South America on his own, figuring that he could return to England in a year.

Then, just as suddenly as the crisis had blown up, it disappeared. Wickham wisely realized that the captain was most worried about the accuracy and completeness of his charts. He reminded FitzRoy that his instructions were only to survey as much of the west coast of South America *as he had time for*. No one expected the charts to be absolutely perfect. Slowly, the captain came around. He would resume command—and they would cross the Pacific.

"For the first time since leaving England," Darwin wrote his sister Catherine, "I now see a clear & not so distant prospect of returning to you all; crossing the Pacific & from Sydney home will not take much time."

As Darwin was still unwell, FitzRoy kindly delayed the *Beagle*'s departure for ten days. Still, the captain was in low spirits and provoked a fight with Darwin for no reason at all. He complained that he was going to have to give a farewell party for their friends in Valparaiso. Darwin suggested that it was not really necessary.

FitzRoy snapped that Darwin was just the sort of man who would receive favors and not return them. Without a word Darwin got up and left the cabin. When he returned to the ship a few days later, the captain was as friendly as ever. They were soon at sea again.

Fire in the Earth

For months, the ship sailed in and out of the islands off the coast of Chile. One day, in a heavy gale, they anchored in a small harbor and took a boat ashore. They were amazed to see a man running toward them on the beach, frantically waving a shirt. He was a castaway! Six deserters from a New England whaling ship had washed ashore more than a year before. Since then, they had been surviving on seal meat, shellfish, and wild celery. "Had it not been for this one chance," Darwin commented, "they might have wandered till they had grown old men, and at last perished on this wild coast."

On January 15, 1835, the ship entered the port of San Carlos on the island of Chiloé. In the middle of the night a few days later, the sentry reported a "large star" on the horizon. Darwin and the other officers rushed on deck. Seventy miles away, Mount Osorno was erupting in a fantastic display of fireworks. Red molten lava and large black rocks spewed brilliantly out of the crater, lighting up sea and sky. Darwin watched for hours, squinting through the telescope. By morning, the volcano was quiet again. The eruption was Darwin's first glimpse of nature at its most violent.

It would not be his last.

Merely a month after watching the volcano erupt, he witnessed an even more devastating display of earth's power. The expedition had progressed north up the coast of Chile to the tumbledown town of Valdivia. On the morning of February 20, while Darwin was exploring a forest, he lay down for a short nap. Suddenly the ground beneath him trembled. It was an earthquake!

When he stood up he felt giddy, "like a person skating over thin ice, which bends under the weight of his body." Though the trembling lasted only two minutes, to Darwin it felt like an eternity.

The experience left him shaken. Now he understood the horror of an earthquake. The earth, the solid dependable earth, actually "moved beneath [the] feet like a thin crust over a fluid." A quake seemed to threaten the security of the planet itself.

None of the trees in the forest fell. But when Darwin rushed back into town, he found damaged buildings and terrified inhabitants.

Valdivia was a small rural town. What kind of destruction had the earthquake caused in the large city of Concepción, 200 miles to the north?

Fourteen days later, the *Beagle* rode into the port of Concepción to find out. Nothing could have prepared Darwin for his first sight of the devastated city. Wood, bricks, furniture, roofs, and bags of cotton lay strewn everywhere, "as if a thousand ships had been wrecked." In the main part of Concepción, which was slightly inland, the foundations of the buildings still stood. But in the port of Talcahuano, even the foundations had been swept away. "Both towns presented the most awful yet interesting spectacle I ever beheld," Darwin said.

From talking to the inhabitants, Darwin pieced together the chronology of that dreadful day. At 11:40 a.m. the first shocks began, opening up cracks in the ground and making a deep thunderous noise. People bolted from their homes and tried to escape into the hills. As houses collapsed around them, horrified men and women clung to trees or tried to climb the piles of rubble that had fallen into the streets. Screaming and crying, they choked on clouds of thick dust and smoke from the fires that burned everywhere. Only two of the massive walls of the great cathedral were still standing. Everyone told him it was Chile's worst earthquake ever.

But the earthquake had just been the beginning. As the ground shook, the seawater retreated from the shore. Every rock and shoal in the bay was visible, and ships at anchor were stranded in the mud. Then, about an hour later, a towering wall of water surged toward the land. It poured into the port with a mighty roar and swept cottages, trees, cattle, horses, sheep—anything that wasn't anchored down—out to sea. Another tidal wave surged in, and then another. Talcahuano was reduced to a flattened wasteland.

Incredibly, only hundreds, rather than thousands,

were killed. After the quake, many people had fled their homes. By the time the giant waves hit, most of them were on higher ground. Still, many people were now homeless and starving. Darwin realized that a natural disaster like this could bankrupt any country—even England—in a matter of minutes.

Dazed as he was, Darwin's scientific curiosity soon took over. To him the most interesting thing about the earthquake was that it had permanently lifted the land out of the sea. In Concepción Bay, the land had been raised two or three feet. And on the island of Santa María, about thirty miles south, FitzRoy found fresh beds of mussel shells ten feet above sea level. Darwin remembered the layers of shells he had seen in the cliffs near Valparaiso and in the Cape Verde Islands. They had somehow been lifted hundreds of feet above sea level. Now he had witnessed with his own eyes how such monumental changes occurred.

Yet even in such a catastrophe, Darwin realized, whole mountains did not suddenly shoot up out of the sea. Instead, the land rose only a few feet at once. It would take endless eons to make a mountain, just as Charles Lyell had theorized. The earth changed steadily but very gradually.

On February 20, Darwin noted, there had also been an earthquake on the island of San Fernandez, 360 miles northeast of Concepción. At the same time, volcanoes had erupted in Chiloé. Somehow, all these events had to be connected. It must be, he decided, that the "forces which slowly and by little starts uplift continents, and those which at successive periods pour forth volcanic matter from open orifices, are identical."

The men of the *Beagle* stayed in the ruined city only three days before returning south to Valparaiso. Now Darwin had just a month to squeeze in his dream journey—to cross the great Andes Mountains. Because winter was coming, he decided to travel by means of the Portilla Pass, which was the closest, although the most dangerous, route. Only sure-footed mules would be able to navigate the narrow and treacherous mountain trails.

Darwin hired a muleteer, together with ten mules and their *madrina*, or "godmother." She was a calm, sturdy mare with a little bell around her neck. Wherever the *madrina* and her tinkling bell went, the other mules would follow. Darwin grew to respect these strong and gentle animals, which could carry more than 300 pounds up a rugged mountain without stumbling.

Up they climbed the steep pass, the atmosphere growing colder and thinner with each step. Every fifty yards the mules would stop to catch their breath, then start again without a signal. Darwin, too, found himself breathing in short gasps. But when he discovered fossil seashells on a high ridge, he forgot his discomfort.

As soon as they reached the summit of the first ridge, 13,000 feet above the sea, Darwin knew it had been worth the struggle. He turned and looked back at the astounding view: the bright blue sky, deep valleys, and majestic peaks with their red and purple rocks and white caps of snow. "I felt glad I was alone," he later reported, "it was like watching a thunderstorm, or hearing in full orchestra a chorus of the *Messiah*."

Darwin and his muleteer crossed over the second ridge of the Andes and gazed down at the flat Argentinean pampas before turning north. They traveled through the fertile valleys of Mendoza, crammed with peach, fig, and olive trees, before reaching the mountain pass that would take them back to Chile.

The thin air and steep, rocky slopes weren't the only dangers Darwin faced on the journey. One night, he awoke in disgust to find a large black vinchuca, an assassin bug, "crawling over his body" and sucking his blood.

The trip back over the Andes, though treacherous, was less frightening for Darwin. By now he felt almost as confident on the narrow mountain paths as did the mules. Jogging along, with yawning chasms a few feet on either side of him, he decided that the danger had been "much exaggerated."

His greatest joy on this return trip was discovering a forest of petrified trees in the mountains. Looking at the "snow white projecting columns," Darwin traced their whole history in his imagination.

On this spot, "a cluster of fine trees once waved their branches on the shores of the Atlantic." The land had apparently collapsed into the sea, where the trees were covered by layers of sand that hardened into rock. Crystallized by the pressure, the trees rose again as underground forces pushed the seabed up into the air. Now they were 7,000 feet above sea level!

To Darwin's delight, he realized that he was building "geological castles in the air."

It was almost time to leave South America forever. Darwin had just a few things left to do: A trip to the rocky desert of northern Chile to Peru. A final shipment of bones and specimens to England. A last night under the stars, drinking an herbal drink called maté and smoking a pipe.

South America had shown Charles Darwin a lot in three-and-a-half years. Volcanoes, earthquakes, petrified forests, huge fossils, and a new species of ostrich.

To what use would he put his experiences in the future? He couldn't even begin to guess.

On September 7, 1835, the *Beagle* set sail from Lima, Peru, en route to a group of islands about 500 miles west. They were the Galápagos, also known as the *Encantatas*, or the "Enchanted Islands."

CHAPTER SEVEN

Lands of the Giant Tortoise
September–October 1835

To the crew of the *Beagle*, the Galápagos Islands looked like a region of hell. Black and barren, they had been formed by lava thrown up by underwater volcanoes. The rocky surface was so hot it scorched their feet through the soles of their boots. Even the air had a hot, sulfurous smell. The islands were home to few types of plants, and even fewer insects and mammals. (Darwin found only a small mouse.) Instead, the fourteen "frying hot" islands had turned into a perfect paradise for reptiles.

Black sand and black lizards met Darwin's eyes when he came ashore on the easternmost island, Chatham. The lizards proved to be marine iguanas, about three feet long, "with a great mouth, and a pouch hanging under it; a kind of horny mane upon the neck and back."

Someone, laughing, called them "imps of darkness." They were agile swimmers, gliding through the water by wiggling their tails and bodies.

Strangely, though, they did not seem to like the water much. Darwin amused himself by grabbing a large iguana by the tail and flinging it into a deep tidal pool. As soon as it splashed in, it scurried out. Each time he threw it in, it was back sunning itself on the rocks within minutes. Maybe the iguana's natural enemies were marine animals like sharks, Darwin guessed. As a result, it tried to avoid the water as much as possible.

A few days after landing on Chatham, Darwin met two of the most ancient inhabitants of the islands— giant tortoises. These huge reptiles lived throughout the Galápagos. In fact the Spanish word *galápago* means "tortoise." With their strange wrinkled heads and alien shapes, Darwin thought, they looked like "inhabitants of some other planet."

At first, the tortoises did not look up as he approached, and Darwin wondered if they might be somewhat deaf. One, calmly chewing on a prickly pear, gave Darwin a long look, then slowly turned and walked away. The other made a loud *hiss!* and quickly pulled his head inside his shell. Darwin threw his arms around the great body, but could not lift it. He estimated that each tortoise must weigh at least 200 pounds.

Lands of the Giant Tortoise

The *Beagle* stopped next at Charles Island, where a colony of Ecuadorean prisoners were being held under the control of an English governor named Nicholas Lawson. The prisoners lived something of a "Robinson Crusoe kind of life," Lawson said, subsisting on home-grown vegetables, pigs, and most importantly, tortoise meat. However, tortoises were becoming scarce on Charles Island. Every whaling ship that stopped killed tortoises for food, sometimes hundreds at a time. Lawson estimated that the giant creature might become extinct within a few decades.

It was Lawson who told Darwin that each one of the Galápagos Islands was home to a different kind of tortoise. Some had dome-shaped shells, he said, and others saddle-shaped shells. Unfortunately, Darwin was not paying much attention to the tortoises at the time. At first he assumed the huge animals were not actually native to these islands but had been brought there by pirates. When the crew of the ship sat down to enjoy a meal of fresh meat or turtle soup, they tossed the shells—and Darwin's future research—overboard!

During his month in the Galápagos, Darwin had ample opportunity to observe the habits of the tortoises. They could grow up to 500 pounds, so big that it took eight to ten men to lift one of them. In such a dry climate, they needed plenty of water. Watering holes were generally found on the top peaks of the islands, where rainwater would collect. Over thousands of years the constant traffic of the tortoises to and from the pools had worn wide paths in the rocks.

Once he followed a group of tortoises up a path. It was like a major highway—thirsty tortoises plodding up the hill and satisfied tortoises coming down. When they reached the pool, the tortoises would plunge their heads into the water, taking long gulps until they had drunk as much as they could. Sometimes they would stay at the top of the hill three or four days, replenishing their water supply. Their bodies could store water for a long time.

Darwin was curious to find out what it was like to ride on one of these great, peaceful beasts. "Frequently," he wrote, "I got on their backs, and then giving a few raps on the hinder parts of their shells, they would rise up and walk away." Their lumbering gait made it almost impossible for him to keep his balance, though. After a few steps, he would fall off.

For a week, Darwin camped out on James Island with Syms Covington and two other men. They had trouble finding a place to pitch their tent because the ground was pocked with iguana burrows. Like their brothers the marine iguanas, land iguanas were exceptionally ugly, with brownish red backs and yellowish orange bellies. They looked like fierce dragons, but were actually peaceful plant eaters.

Darwin was fascinated to watch them dig their burrows. First, they dug furiously with the front and back claws on one side of their bodies. Then they would scrape and scoop with the claws on the other side. Once Darwin waited until an iguana had almost finished its hole and yanked on its tail. The iguana whipped around and stared the intruder full in the face. "What made you pull my tail?" its expression seemed to say.

Darwin spent much of the last week and a half of their stay in the Galápagos on James Island, collecting as many specimens of birds and plants as he could. In all, he reported proudly, he shot twenty-six kinds of land birds and eleven seabirds. Of the twenty-six, he judged, twenty-five were new species. Early on, he could tell that each island had its own species of mockingbird. He obtained samples from four islands and labeled them carefully.

Finches, though, were the most numerous birds on the islands. They flocked in the tall grasses, pecking at the seeds lying on the ground. When Darwin approached, the birds took off together in a flurry of dark wings. They looked like ordinary finches, with brown, black, or greenish feathers, but Darwin found them confusing. Were the brown finches of a different species than the black ones? Were the bigger finches a different species than the smaller ones? He couldn't tell.

Altogether, Darwin shot and collected six different types of finches from three different islands. In his hurry, he not only mixed two different types together in his samples, but he also mislabeled them. Luckily, Captain FitzRoy and other members of the crew had also collected and identified samples that Darwin could use for future research.

A few months after he left the Galápagos, Darwin wrote in his diary, "When I see these islands in sight of each other, possessed of but a scanty stock of animals, tenanted by these birds, but slightly differing in structure and filling the same place in Nature, I must suspect they are only varieties."

Darwin didn't learn what he had found until he got back to England and asked an ornithologist to examine the finches from the islands. In 1839, he wrote that there were thirteen different species of ground finches in the Galápagos, distinguished not by their feathers, but by the size of their beaks. The beaks ranged from "extraordinarily thick" to "very fine." Not only that, but each species had its own island!

Lands of the Giant Tortoise

Modern researchers have confirmed that the finches' beak size depends on the food source on each particular island. On the islands where the main food is hard seeds, the finches have large, strong beaks. On the islands where the finches eat mainly cactus fruits, they have smaller, narrower beaks. Each species of finch has adapted to survive on the food available to it.

The Galápagos Islands are famous today because they represent a change in Darwin's thinking. When he published *The Voyage of the Beagle* in 1839, he was able to report that "by far the most remarkable feature in the natural history of this archipelago…is that the different islands to a considerable extent are inhabited by a different set of beings." This applied to tortoises, mockingbirds, finches, and plants. Most extraordinary to Darwin was that all varieties of each type of animal had the same habits and occupied the same ecological niche. Why was there so much variety within a small group of islands? And how did animals and plants arrive on this group of volcanic islands to begin with? After all, Darwin wrote, the islands had "risen out of the ocean fairly recently, in geological terms. Hence, both in space and time, we seem to be brought somewhat near to that great fact—that mystery of mysteries—the first appearance of new beings on this earth."

Charles Darwin was full of questions, but he had no answers yet.

As the *Beagle* left the Galápagos on October 20, the seamen brought aboard eighteen live tortoises as food for the long trip. Darwin and Covington, however, took with them three tortoise babies—to be studied, not eaten.

Next on the agenda: a 3,200-mile trip across the Pacific Ocean.

CHAPTER EIGHT
Homeward Bound
October 21, 1835–October 2, 1836

The passengers of the *Beagle* were in a holiday mood as the ship skimmed across the wide ocean. The main mission of their voyage, surveying the South American coast, had been completed. The only task remaining for Captain FitzRoy was to calculate the longitude of various places around the globe. In the meantime, the sun shone brilliantly, the water glistened, and exotic lands awaited: Tahiti, New Zealand, and Australia.

For twenty-five days, Darwin hunkered down in the poop cabin, dissecting, labeling, and recording his observations. Writing was harder than he had thought, he complained in a letter to his sisters: "I am just now beginning to discover the difficulty of expressing one's ideas on paper. As long as it consists solely of description it is pretty easy, but where reasoning comes into play…[it] is to me, as I have said, a difficulty of which I had no idea." His queasy stomach made him grumpy, too. Even now, four years into the voyage, he remained a "martyr to sea-sickness."

But at least, as he wrote in his diary, "every league…which we travel onwards, is one league nearer to England."

The beautiful island of Tahiti immediately cheered him up. When their ship anchored in Matavai Bay on November 15, canoes full of "laughing merry" Tahitians came out to greet it. British missionaries had converted the Tahitians to Christianity about thirty years earlier, and Darwin was pleased to see them respectably dressed in loincloths and even shirts. The men, he noticed, sported elegant tattoos. He especially admired a palm tree pattern on their backs that "gracefully curled around both sides." He was less approving of the women, who shaved the crown of their heads and let the hair on the sides hang straight. Why? he asked himself. Because "it is the fashion & that is the answer enough at Tahiti as well as Paris."

Naturally, he insisted on exploring the lush tropical landscape. With two native guides, Darwin and Syms Covington set off down a riverbed bordered by cliffs that soared thousands of feet into the air. They climbed up a sheer face by means of ropes dangling down from a rocky ledge. As Darwin pulled himself up, ferns and lilies blocked his view of the ravine below. Otherwise, Darwin admitted, he would never have dared make the ascent.

At night, the guides cut down bamboo stalks and banana leaves to fashion a makeshift hut. They dove into the river "like otters [and] with eyes open followed the fish into holes and corners and thus caught them." The Tahitians wrapped the strips of fish and banana in leaves and baked them between hot stones. In Tahiti, Darwin discovered, it was actually possible to live off the land. Delicious meals of pineapples, coconuts, oranges, and breadfruit practically fell from the trees.

One night Pomare, the queen of Tahiti, came aboard the *Beagle* for dinner. The ship, bedecked with bright nautical flags, was decorated for royalty. Darwin found the queen herself "large and awkward," with a permanently sulky expression. She only came to life when the ship's crew lit up the sky with a brilliant burst of rockets.

On December 3, after just three weeks in this island paradise, the *Beagle* set sail again, en route for New Zealand. Darwin found the land a disappointment after Tahiti. He had admired the Tahitians for their beauty and their polite, cheerful manners. The Maori natives, by contrast, appeared mean and unfriendly. When the English had first arrived in 1770, they found warlike cannibals. Explorer Captain James Cook recorded that when his ship first neared the New Zealand coast, the Maoris threw stones at it and shouted in their language, "Come on shore, and we will kill and eat you all!"

The tattoos that covered the Maoris made them look particularly "horrid and ferocious," in Darwin's opinion. Male and females alike decorated their faces with black symmetrical lines cut in complicated patterns. The cuts healed and froze the muscles, so that their faces had a set, rigid look. Some looked almost like demons.

Darwin was not sorry to leave New Zealand and strike out for Australia after just nine days. But again he was disappointed. In 1835, Australia was still a penal colony, a continent-wide prison where Britain sent its convicted thieves and debtors. Gangs of slave convict laborers worked on the sheep farms and on the paved roads. Darwin couldn't help but pity the convicts for their slave status. Yet he was repelled by their vicious habits. How could Australia grow to be a great country, he wondered, inhabited as it was by such immoral people?

Homeward Bound

He liked the friendly Aborigines, the original native Australians. Once, on King George Sound, he watched a dancing party called a "corrobery." The "White Cockatoo men" and "King George's men" painted themselves with white spots and lines and stamped up and down, beating their clubs and spears together in the light of a great fire. In the emu dance, each man stretched out one bent arm like the neck of the bird. In the kangaroo dance, one man pretended to graze peacefully while a hunter crept up behind him with a spear. At the end of the performance, all the participants were presented with a feast of boiled rice and sugar.

Tragically, the number of Aborigines seemed to be decreasing. The white men's plagues—disease, alcohol, and the extinction of prey animals—had already taken their toll. As Darwin himself witnessed, "Wherever the European has trod death seems to pursue the aboriginal. From Polynesia to North and South America, to New Zealand and Australia, it is the same." He saw an obvious parallel between human behavior and that of other animals: "The Varieties of man seem to act on each other in the same way as different species of animals—the stronger always [destroying] the weaker."

He was horrified to learn that on the nearby island of

Tasmania, settlers had wiped out almost all of the natives. Only 210 of the original inhabitants remained.

Unfortunately, Darwin saw few of Australia's unique animals. Although he went kangaroo hunting, he never spotted an actual kangaroo. English greyhounds brought by the settlers had hunted and killed all the native kangaroos in the area. The only marsupial (a mammal whose young mature in a pouch outside the mother's body) he saw was a kangaroo rat caught by some dogs. He did have the chance to observe several weird-looking, web-footed duck-billed platypuses, though. When a hunter killed one for him to examine, Darwin exclaimed, "I think it a great feat, to be in at the death of so wonderful an animal."

His stay in Australia was brief. "Farewell Australia," he wrote in his journal when the time came to leave. "You are too great and ambitious for affection, yet not great enough for respect; I leave your shores without sorrow or regret."

By then, all Darwin could think about was going home. By March 1836, he had been away from England for four years and three months. It had been thirteen months since he had received a letter from his family, although he kept posting his own from every port of call. "I never see a Merchant vessel start for England without a most dangerous inclination to bolt," he confessed to his sisters. "I feel inclined to write about nothing else but to tell you, over and over again, how I long to be quietly seated among you."

He had another long nine months to wait, as the *Beagle* continued swinging west across the Pacific. But each stop offered Darwin new experiences. On the Cocos Islands in the Indian Ocean, he made the acquaintance of some coconut-eating crabs. The relationship between crab and coconut was "As curious a case as ever I heard...of adaptation in structure between two objects so remote from each other in the scheme of nature," he noted. On the French-speaking island of Mauritius, he rode on the back of an elephant. On the island of St. Helena, he visited Napoleon's tomb.

In Capetown, South Africa, Darwin welcomed the opportunity to meet the great English astronomer, John Herschel. Herschel, too, was fascinated by Charles Lyell's notion of gradual geological change. Like Darwin, he accepted the theory and took it a step further. If all the continents on earth change gradually, Herschel wondered, then why not species of animals? Weren't new species as natural as new rock formations?

It was a question Darwin was pondering as well.

In Capetown, Darwin's letters from England finally caught up with him. And what wonderful news they contained! Henslow had published Darwin's letters on South American geology and distributed the booklet to British scientists. When Darwin finally set foot on English shores, his reputation would precede him.

But when would that be? The crew was elated when they rounded the Cape of Good Hope at the tip of Africa and headed north in the Atlantic. Surely they would speed straight to England.

But no. To their horror, Captain FitzRoy set course for South America once more. In order to make accurate longitudinal reckonings, he wanted to completely encircle the globe. So it was back to Bahia in Brazil.

"There never was a ship so full of homesick heroes as the 'Beagle,'" according to Darwin. They spent seven long days in Brazil before heading back across the Atlantic.

He made good use of his time by writing out catalogs of all his collections—which totaled 1,529 species preserved in alcohol and 3,907 separate specimens of animal skin, bones, feathers, etc. In addition, Darwin had written a 70-page diary, a 1,388-page manuscript on geology, and 368 pages of notes on zoology. Here was more than enough raw material for a lifetime of study and scholarship.

And he now had questions to go with his collections and observations. What forces caused changes in the earth? Why did megatheriums and other extinct animals die out? Why were the animals on the Galápagos Islands different species, yet closely related? How did the animals arrive on the islands? Why were human beings—Fuegians and Tahitians and Maoris and Aborigines and Englishmen—all so different, even though they were of the same species?

Above all, how did species come into existence and how did they become extinct?

The answers would have to wait. In the meantime, the *Beagle* shot north—across the equator, through the Cape Verde Islands, past North Africa, and around Spain. Finally, in the early hours of the morning of October 2, 1836, Charles Darwin peered through the rain and sighted the coast of England.

CHAPTER NINE
Toward an Origin of Species

Darwin was home at last. The coach bumping over the English roads was hot and crowded, but he was in no mood to complain. At last he was going to see his family.

As soon as the *Beagle* moored in Falmouth Harbor, he had boarded a mail coach to take him to Shrewsbury. The journey took two days of nonstop travel. But to Darwin, everything looked "beautiful and cheerful!" There was no place like England.

He reached The Mount in the dead of night. Rather than wake anyone, he slipped into his own bedroom for a snooze. The next morning, he came down to breakfast—and gave his family the surprise of their lives! After hugs and kisses, his sisters agreed that Darwin looked quite healthy, if a bit too thin. His father, though, exclaimed, "Why, the shape of his head is quite altered!"

More had changed than just the shape of Darwin's head. No longer an uncertain schoolboy, he had become a strong, self-confident man and a respected scientist. Instead of a cause of anxiety to his father, he was now a source of pride. Charles boasted to FitzRoy that "I am a very great man at home—the five years' voyage has certainly raised me a hundred percent."

However, Darwin could not rest on his laurels. He had no time to lose—he had dozens of boxes of specimens that needed to be examined by the best botanists, zoologists, and geologists in England.

The next two years were a frenzy of activity. First he moved to London, so he could meet the most important scientists in the country and get all his projects off the ground.

The birds would go to one specialist, the reptiles to another, the insects and mammals to a third. The plants he sent to John Henslow at Cambridge, the first friend he visited after his return.

The fossils ended up with Richard Owen, an up-and-coming anatomist at the College of Surgeons in London. It was he who confirmed that the grazing rhinoceros-like animal was a Toxodon. The giant ground sloth was a new species he named *Scelidotherium*. (A few years later, in 1841, Owen would be the one to give the definitive name to a group of extinct reptiles: dinosaurs, or "terrible lizards.")

The most important and lasting of Charles's new friends was Charles Lyell, the writer of *Principles of Geology*. Lyell was particularly eager to meet his disciple, and Darwin found that Lyell had "the most good-natured manner."

Darwin also began writing his account of his trip around the world, *The Journal of the Voyage of the Beagle,* first published in 1839. He edited five volumes on the zoology of the voyage, and was made secretary of the Royal Geological Society. The biggest changes in his life, however, were personal.

Darwin had long been friends with his cousin Emma Wedgwood, one year older than he. Emma was well educated, fluent in several languages, and talented at archery and the piano. She was everything a wife should be—intelligent, sympathetic, and rich. Yet Darwin feared that marriage would rob him of precious time to study. Should he marry or not? He wrote out the pros and cons:

Marry:
Children—(if it please God)
Constant companion (& friend in old age)
Home, & someone to take care of house

These things good for one's health—*but*
terrible loss of time
Not Marry:
Freedom to go where one liked
Choice of society & *little of it*
More money for books

Finally, the pros won out. He hated the thought of being alone all his life, "spending one's whole life like a neuter bee, working, working, & nothing at all—No, no, it won't do."

Clearly marriage was the better choice. So he steeled himself against possible rejection and proposed to Emma on November 11, 1838. To his intense delight, she accepted.

They were married two months later and set up housekeeping, first in London, then in Down House in Kent, sixteen miles outside the city. Children followed immediately: William Erasmus in December 1839, and Anne Elizabeth in March 1841.

Altogether, Charles and Emma had ten children over a period of seventeen years, two of whom died in infancy. Darwin's darling, his eldest daughter Annie, died when she was just ten years old. He mourned her all his life.

Toward an Origin of Species

In good times and bad, Emma proved to be a true and faithful wife. Charles was a kind and devoted husband, loving toward his children and happy to be surrounded by the comforts of home. Emma praised her husband as "the most open, transparent man I ever saw, and every word expresses his real thoughts. He is particularly affectionate and nice to his father and sisters, and perfectly sweet-tempered, and possesses some minor qualities that add particularly to one's happiness—such as being humane to animals."

Of Emma, Charles wrote, "More than any woman I ever knew, she *comforted*." And Charles was in need of comfort, because he spent the next forty years battling a mysterious ailment.

No one has ever pinpointed the cause of Darwin's illness. Some scholars have suggested that he picked up a chronic infection while he was in South America. Perhaps it was Chagas' disease, contracted from the assassin bug. Or maybe it was caused in part by the constant stress of his research. Whatever it was, he suffered from recurring stomach cramps, headaches, weakness, and fatigue. His son Francis remembered that "for nearly forty years, he never knew one day of the health of ordinary men, and thus his life was one long struggle against the weariness and strain of sickness."

What we do know is that this world traveler never again left England. Darwin rarely, indeed, left his home, except to visit relatives or spas where he would undergo "water cures." Luckily for Charles, he did not have to earn a living for his growing family. Both his and Emma's wealthy fathers guaranteed them an income when they were married, and they were set for life. Darwin never had to earn a salary—never had to carry out the duties of either clergyman or doctor, the professions he had once considered. Instead, he became what he had always wanted to be—a full-time naturalist.

In spite of his illness, on weekdays and weekends alike, Charles kept the same schedule for the rest of his life. In the morning, he conducted experiments and wrote. In the afternoon, he walked, read, and spent time with his family. Like all scientists, he conducted experiments and collected facts. But what made Darwin different from other scientists—what made him a genius—was the way he used the facts he collected to generalize about the natural world. In particular, he tried to solve the question that had nagged at him since he paced the decks of the *Beagle*. How were species born and how did they die?

"On July 1837 I opened my first notebook for facts in relation to the Origin of the Species," he wrote a friend, "about which I had long reflected, and never ceased working for the next twenty years."

His observations during the long voyage had convinced Darwin that living organisms changed, or evolved, over time. The idea of evolution itself was not new. His grandfather Erasmus Darwin had proposed that all living things descended from a common ancestor and that species changed as they adapted to their surroundings. In 1801, French biologist Jean-Baptiste Lamarck had proposed that individual creatures acquired traits during their lifetimes that they could pass on to their offspring. For instance, by stretching to reach fruit high in the treetops, a giraffe could lengthen its neck—and pass the longer neck on to its children. Darwin agreed that traits were passed from one generation to the next, but he proposed a different mechanism for the transmittal of the traits.

For twenty years, he gathered and analyzed evidence about how such change occurred. Since all species descended through reproduction, and no offspring was exactly like its parent, Darwin concluded that change must occur in the process of reproduction. He called the process "descent with modification."

The thirteen species of finches on the Galápagos, for instance, were very similar and belonged to the same group of birds. Yet finches on separate islands had different kinds of beaks, adapted for different kinds of food. Darwin was convinced that they all descended from common ancestors and had developed different beaks depending on their environment. Probably the earliest ancestor of the finches had flown from South America to the volcanic islands after they rose from the ocean.

By 1838, just a year after he opened his notebook, Darwin had figured out the central idea of evolution, what he called "natural selection." In all species of animals and plants, more offspring were produced than could possibly survive to maturity. Naturally, only those that were best adapted to the changing environment would survive. In each species, individuals were involved in a "struggle for existence," competing with each other for valuable space and food supplies. The weaker or more vulnerable might be killed off by environmental factors such as predators, disease, and famine.

Yet particular traits might also increase an individual's ability to survive in a given environment. Characteristics such as size, strength, intelligence, speed, or resistance to disease might give certain individuals an advantage. Since those who survived were most likely to reproduce, their offspring inherited their traits. Over time, more and more individuals would possess the traits favorable to their particular environment. Within thousands of generations, variations would make one population differ so much from another population that they would become two separate species. This would explain how Galápagos finches on Chatham Island, for instance, would be a separate species from the finches on James Island.

To sum up, Darwin stated: "As many more individuals of each species are born than can possibly survive, and as consequently there is a frequently recurring struggle for existence, it follows that any being, if it vary however slightly in any manner profitable to itself…will have a better chance of surviving, and thus be naturally selected…. This preservation of favourable individual differences and variations, and the destruction of those which are injurious, I have called Natural Selection, or the Survival of the Fittest."

Because Darwin knew that his theory of evolution was so revolutionary, he tried to back it up with as much evidence as possible. For example, he studied how English cattle breeders consciously selected cows and bulls with desirable characteristics to mate and produce offspring. These offspring had a greater chance of having those characteristics, which they would then pass on to others. Such artificial breeding, he insisted, had its parallel in natural selection.

Darwin was in no hurry to publish his findings. When he did, he wanted his argument to be as airtight as possible. In 1844, he wrote a short explanation of his theory and sent it to his good friends Charles Lyell and botanist Joseph Hooker.

Even so, he was unprepared when another world traveler and amateur naturalist sent him a letter on June 18, 1858. Young Alfred Russel Wallace wrote Darwin that he had discovered how evolution worked. Darwin was appalled. Wallace had reached essentially the same conclusions he had.

If Wallace were to publish first, Wallace, not Darwin, would be credited with the idea of evolution.

"All my originality, whatever it may come to, will be smashed!" Darwin wrote to Charles Lyell in utter desperation.

Hastily Darwin's friends came up with a plan. Lyell and Hooker sent Wallace's essay and Darwin's outline of 1844 to the famous scientific organization the Linnean Society. Hooker explained to the members that he had read Darwin's essay ten years before, convincing them that Darwin's ideas had preceded Wallace's. Therefore, although Wallace and Darwin would share credit for the idea of evolution, Darwin was firmly established as the originator of the theory.

For years, Darwin had been slowly and methodically writing up his findings. Now he went into high gear, busily scribbling as fast as possible. In March 1859, he sent his manuscript to his publisher in London.

His magnum opus—the fruit of nearly thirty years of labor—was published in November 1859. It was titled *On the Origin of Species by Means of Natural Selection.* To future generations, it has been known simply as *On the Origin of Species.*

The age of modern biology had arrived.

CHAPTER TEN
A Glory to His Country

On Wednesday, April 26, 1882, the bells of Westminster Abbey tolled as a funeral procession slowly wound its way into the cathedral. The Abbey was the royal tomb of kings, queens, and prime ministers, and it was also the final resting place for Britain's greatest writers, composers, and scientists, including Geoffrey Chaucer, George Frideric Handel, Charles Dickens, and Sir Isaac Newton. Now another illustrious figure would be buried under the ancient stones: Charles Darwin.

It had been twenty-three years since the publication of the groundbreaking *On the Origin of Species.* In that time, Darwin had become one of the most famous men in all England, indeed, in the entire world. The book had burst upon the scene like a thunderclap. Thousands of people read it, and every reader had an opinion.

Within months the book had gone into a second, third, and fourth printing. Some scholars attempted to disprove Darwin's central thesis that all life was in a constant process of change. Others found Darwin's evidence and arguments forceful and indisputable. By 1863, the Reverend Charles Kingsley could report that "Darwin is conquering everywhere and rushing in like a flood, by the mere force of truth and fact."

For all the uproar over his work, Darwin's daily life changed very little. While others fought battles on his behalf, he remained at Down House, conducting experiments and puttering in the garden. His father died, his children grew up, and Darwin's beard grew long and gray. His health remained so uncertain that he rarely went to scientific meetings or lectures. Admirers had to make the pilgrimage to Down House to talk to the great man.

Every day he picked up his walking stick and took a long stroll on the Sandwalk, a pebbly path he had built through his property. It was here that Darwin did most of his thinking.

Much of Darwin's work at this time—on worms, on insectivorous (insect-eating) plants, and on climbing plants—was based upon studies he made in his own garden. Yet he did write another book on evolution,

A Glory to His Country

The Descent of Man, in 1871. It attempted to demonstrate that human beings, too, had evolved from earlier, less complex creatures, and that the brain could also change by means of natural selection. He never suggested that humans had evolved from apes. Rather, he said, humans and apes alike were descended from a common, more ancient ancestor.

By the time Charles Darwin died from heart disease on April 19, 1882, he was an English institution. The funeral at the Abbey reflected public pride in his revolutionary ideas and scientific accomplishments. At the height of the Victorian era, Darwin's life and work seemed to symbolize British success in controlling nature and conquering the globe. With his death, the *Pall Mall Gazette* exclaimed, Great Britain had "lost a man whose name is a glory to his country."

The young man who set foot on the ship HMS *Beagle* fifty-two years before could never have imagined where his voyage of discovery would take him. It had truly been the trip of a lifetime.

Bibliography

Browne, Janet. *Charles Darwin: Voyaging.* New York: Knopf, 1995.

Darwin, Charles. *On the Origin of Species.* Reprint. New York: Signet Classics, 2003.

Darwin, Charles. *The Voyage of the* Beagle. Reprint. New York: The Modern Library, 2001.

Desmond, Adrian, and James Moore. *Darwin: The Life of a Tormented Evolutionist.* New York: Warner Books, 1991.

Eldredge, Niles. *Darwin: Discovering the Tree of Life.* New York: Norton, 2005.

Irvine, William. *Apes, Angels, and Victorians: The Story of Darwin, Huxley, and Evolution.* New York: McGraw Hill, 1955.

Keynes, Richard Darwin. *Fossils, Finches and Fuegians: Charles Darwin's Adventures and Discoveries on the* Beagle, *1832–1836.* Oxford: Oxford University Press, 2003.

Nardo, Don. *The Origin of Species: Darwin's Theory of Evolution.* San Diego: Lucent Books, 2001.

Moorhead, Alan. *Darwin and the* Beagle. New York: Harper & Row, 1969.

For Further Reading

Gibbons, Alan. *Charles Darwin.* Kingfisher, 2008.

Heiligman, Deborah. *Charles and Emma: The Darwins' Leap of Faith.* New York: Henry Holt, 2008.

Hopkinson, Deborah. *Who Was Charles Darwin?* New York: Grosset & Dunlap, 2005.

King, David C. *Charles Darwin.* New York: DK Books, 2006.

Lawson, Kristan. *Darwin and Evolution for Kids: His Life and Ideas with 21 Activities.* Chicago: Chicago Review Press, 2003.

MacDonald, Fiona. *Inside the* Beagle *with Charles Darwin.* Enchanted Lion Books, 2005.

Sís, Peter. *The Tree of Life: Darwin.* New York: Farrar, Straus, & Giroux, 2003.

Stefoff, Rebecca. *Charles Darwin and the Evolution Revolution.* Oxford: Oxford University Press, 1996.

Author's Note

Charles Darwin and His Time

Charles Darwin lived in an age of rapid change and extraordinary scientific progress. During that time, inventors came up with the steam locomotive, an early computer, the telegraph, the sewing machine, the internal combustion engine, the electric light, dynamite, and photography. Scientists and doctors first gave an anesthetic, created a theory of germs, performed antiseptic surgery, composed the periodic table of the elements, and discovered the germ that caused tuberculosis. For the first time, people rode bicycles, typed letters, and spoke into microphones.

sewing machine

electric lamp

It was a time of daily change, not just in the way people lived, but in the way they thought. Discoveries in geology and paleontology led people to reimagine earth's place in the universe. When Darwin was born in 1809, most Englishmen believed that the earth was around 6,000 years old and that human beings had existed for most of that time. By the time Darwin died, scientists had shown that the earth was much, much older—perhaps millions, or even billions, of years old. The exact age of the earth couldn't be calculated until the next century.

Charles Darwin in his later years

Darwin's theory of the evolution of all species was based in part on the work of other scientists. Here is a timeline of some of the discoveries that were made shortly before the publication of *On the Origin of Species*

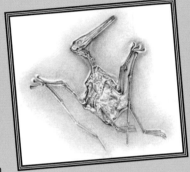

Pterodactyl fossil

Monsters in the Rocks

1796—Ancient elephant bones are dug up in Paris. French scientist Georges Cuvier announces that because the bones do not match those of living elephants, they must be those of a prehistoric species of elephant—an *extinct* species, or one that no longer exists. For the first time, science recognizes that all species of living things are not created—and do not die out—at the same time.

Cuvier and other paleontologists also identify fossils of other extinct species, including a huge sea lizard they named *Mosasaurus* and a flying reptile called a pterodactyl.

1796—Surveyor William Smith studies the strata, or different layers, of the earth in England. His observations show that the lower the layer, the more ancient the rock. He also announces that fossils buried in a particular layer are from the same time period as the rock. In other words, studying fossils now gives scientists a new way to measure time.

Engraving from William Smith's guide to classifying rock strata by characteristic fossils, published in 1815

1812—Cuvier publishes a theory on the earth's history. He says that violent events such as earthquakes, volcanoes, floods, and glaciers changed the surface of the earth and caused the extinction of plants and animals. "Living things without number were swept out of existence by the catastrophes," he declares.

1822—Mary Ann Mantell discovers what looks like a large tooth in sandstone rock in the south of England. Her husband Gideon Mantell identifies it as the tooth of a huge plant-eating reptile. He calls the creature *Iguanodon*— "iguana tooth."

1824—Fossil hunter William Buckland announces the discovery of the fossil remains of an extinct giant flesh-eating reptile he calls *Megalosaurus*. Like *Iguanodon, Megalosaurus* is a strange, unfamiliar animal. Other exciting finds include *Thecodontosaurus, Palaeosaurus,* and *Plateosaurus.*

Illustration of *Iguanodon* teeth by Gideon Mantell, 1825

1830–1833—Charles Lyell publishes the three-volume work *Principles of Geology,* which challenges Cuvier's theory of catastrophic change. Lyell states that the earth does not change quickly over a short period of time. It changes, he claims, very slowly over a very long period of time.

1841—Richard Owen coins a new name for the mysterious reptiles. He calls them dinosaurs, from the Greek words *deinos,* meaning "terrible," and *sauros,* meaning "lizard."

1854—For the Crystal Palace exhibit in London, sculptor Waterhouse Hawkins creates life-size sculptures of three dinosaurs: *Iguanodon, Megalosaurus,* and *Hylaeosaurus.* He mistakenly places Mantell's "tooth" on top of *Iguanodon's* head, thinking it must have been a horn. Today we know the bony structure wasn't a tooth or a horn but was actually a thumb spike! Dinosaurs become *very* popular in England.

1859—Charles Darwin publishes *On the Origin of Species.*

The Oxford Debate

By the time Darwin wrote *On the Origin of Species,* most scientists accepted the fact that species regularly become extinct and new species regularly come into existence. Nonetheless, his theory of natural selection caused an uproar. Some people could not believe that the earth was much more ancient than the 6,000 years the Bible seemed to suggest. Some were disturbed by the thought that all of nature was caught up in a violent "survival-of-the-fittest" struggle. And some were horrified by the idea that human beings were descended from more primitive life forms.

Luckily, Darwin had his three best friends to help him explain his theory to the world: botanist Joseph Hooker, geologist Charles Lyell, and biologist Thomas Huxley. Huxley became known as "Darwin's Bulldog" because he vigorously defended his friend against all attackers.

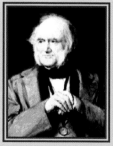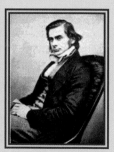

Joseph Hooker, Charles Lyell, and Thomas Huxley

On June 28, 1860, opponents and supporters of Darwin's theory confronted one another at a meeting of the British Association for the Advancement of Science at Oxford University. The anti-Darwinist group was led by Samuel

Wilberforce, an Anglican bishop who knew little about science. The pro-Darwinists were led by Huxley and Hooker. Darwin, ill at home, didn't attend the meeting.

Samuel Wilberforce

Wilberforce spoke first, making fun of Darwin's ideas. He mocked evolution, pointing out that no one with their very own eyes had ever seen plants or animals changing. Could a turnip someday evolve into a human being? he joked. Looking straight at Huxley, he asked whether Huxley was descended from apes on his grandmother's or on his grandfather's side!

"A man has no reason to be ashamed of having an ape for his grandfather," Huxley shot back. Better an ape, he argued, than a man like Wilberforce who didn't know what he was talking about.

The crowd roared in appreciation. People on opposing sides started shouting at one another. Only Joseph Hooker, who gave a reasoned support of evolution, was able to calm them down. By the end of the meeting, it was Wilberforce who looked foolish, not Darwin. Nonetheless, the Oxford meeting did not end the debate over evolution.

A Missing Link?

The anti-Darwinists argued that Darwin could not prove his theory of evolution because no one had ever observed one species evolving into another. If his theory was correct, they reasoned, there must be fossils

Archaeopteryx fossil

that represent "missing links" between two species. Two years after the publication of *Origin,* stonecutters in Bavaria found fossils from a reptile-bird that seemed to fit the bill. *Archaeopteryx* had feathers, little pointed teeth, and a long reptilian tail. Darwin had suggested that birds were descended from dinosaurs. *Archaeopteryx* was the kind of in-between species he had predicted.

After the *Beagle*

For Darwin, life after his exciting adventure would bring marriage, children, and eventual fame. His shipmates fared differently. Here's what awaited some of his fellow travelers:

Charles Darwin as a young man

Emma Darwin

Syms Covington remained as Darwin's faithful servant and secretary until 1838, when he emigrated to Australia and worked in the gold mines. Covington and Darwin corresponded until Covington's death in 1861.

Robert FitzRoy and Darwin stayed friends for many years, though they saw each other less often as time went on. The conservative captain did not approve of Darwin's theory of natural selection. In 1854 he became the first weather forecaster in British history.

But trying to predict the weather was a chancy business. FitzRoy was criticized for inaccuracy and gave in to despair. On April 30, 1865, suffering from depression and deeply in debt, he committed suicide.

York Minster married Fuegia Basket. In about 1837, he was killed in revenge for the slaying of another man.

Jemmy Button hailed a British ship in Ponsonby Sound twenty-two years after the *Beagle* left him on the shore. "Jam-mes Button, me; where's the ladder?" he called out. He asked for a pair of trousers and had dinner with the ship's captain. Over the next few years he acted as translator for British missionaries who had arrived to convert the Fuegians. In 1859, the missionaries were massacred. Whether Jemmy knew of the attack ahead of time or tried to prevent it, no one knows. He died in 1864, probably of measles.

Fuegia Basket became York Minster's wife and had two children by him. In 1873, an Englishman in Tierra del Fuego found her still strong and hearty, with a much-younger husband. She could still speak a few words of English. Ten years later, when he met her for the last time, she was sixty-two and looked quite frail. When the *Beagle* arrived in Tierra del Fuego in 1833, about 8,000 Fuegians were living there. By the end of the century, only 200 remained. Disease brought by the white man had wiped out the rest.

The Face on the Ten-Pound Note

Two hundred years after his birth, Charles Darwin is still in the news. His revolutionary ideas, the basis of modern biology, are more important—and for some, more controversial—than ever. In 2000, Darwin's face replaced that

A British ten-pound note

of novelist Charles Dickens on the British ten-pound note. Behind Darwin's figure, HMS *Beagle* sails over the horizon in search of new adventure. Today the voyage of the *Beagle* stands for the spirit of discovery that keeps scientists on a never-ending quest for knowledge. And Charles Darwin himself has entered the twenty-first century with a reputation as one of the most important thinkers of all time.

HMS *Beagle*